Charles John Ellicott

The Destiny of the Creature, and Other Sermons

Preached before the University of Cambridge

Charles John Ellicott

The Destiny of the Creature, and Other Sermons
Preached before the University of Cambridge

ISBN/EAN: 9783337036409

Printed in Europe, USA, Canada, Australia, Japan

Cover: Foto ©Lupo / pixelio.de

More available books at **www.hansebooks.com**

THE
DESTINY OF THE CREATURE:

AND

OTHER SERMONS.

PREACHED BEFORE THE UNIVERSITY OF CAMBRIDGE.

BY

CHARLES J. ELLICOTT, B.D.,

DEAN OF EXETER, AND PROFESSOR OF DIVINITY, KING'S COLLEGE,
LONDON.

SECOND EDITION.

LONDON:
PARKER, SON, AND BOURN, WEST STRAND.
1862.

LONDON:
SAVILL AND EDWARDS, PRINTERS, CHANDOS STREET,
COVENT GARDEN.

PREFACE.

THE first four of the following sermons were preached by me before the University of Cambridge during the month of March, 1858, in the capacity of Select Preacher for that month. The fifth and sixth sermons were preached before the same honourable audience, the former in the morning of one of the Sundays in Lent, 1856, on one of the turns of my own College; the latter on the morning of Commencement Sunday, 1857, at the request of the Vice-chancellor. These two sermons are here added, partly in tardy compliance with a wish expressed at the time that they should be published, partly, and more especially, because they both illustrate, and are illustrated by, the Course with which they are associated. On the suggestion of friends, a few hastily gathered notes are appended to the whole; as it was considered that the subjects which are here discussed are all of a kind that require this further mode of illustration. In justice, however, to myself, I feel it right to say, that as the sermons were not written with a view to publication, no record was kept of the many sources from which the opinions expressed in them were derived. The notes, therefore, must be regarded, and kindly allowed for, as simply illustrative collections and reminiscences of mere general reading, rather than as the results of a definite course of study, of which the sermons might be considered the exponents. They are, I am well aware, very incomplete; still they may, perhaps, serve their purpose, which is only that of interesting the general reader, and of directing the student to sources of information from which he may complete and fill in what in the sermons is only imperfect and in outline.

As to the sermons, they must speak for themselves. They are all on subjects of great moment, and attempt to give a few faltering answers to questions that I verily believe are almost daily rising up in the hearts of most of the earnest thinkers of our own time; but which, nevertheless, by a kind of common consent, are either at once repressed, or only answered with a temerity which too often places its own intuitions in undisguised antagonism to the written word of God. I am well aware that the answers that I have presumed to make will provoke much criticism. It will be, not improbably, urged, that the interpretations of Scripture on which these sermons are based are narrow and bibliolatrous; their deductions chimerically literal; that their general views of life are depressing and melancholy; that they speak of nought but obstructions and retardations, where all is buoyancy and progress; that they see only unreal and sentimental shadows, where all is vivid and exhilarating sunshine. Be it so. I have neither the will nor the ability to enter into controversy; but this only will I say, that I would sooner trust the results of an honest, fair, *yet awed* interpretation of Scripture, than the mere plausibilities of a specious Philosophy. Nay, I am old-fashioned enough to be fully persuaded, that if modern thinkers lent an ear to the express declarations of Inspiration as readily as they do to the deductions of philosophy—if we perused the Book of Life as studiously and as dutifully as we do the Book of Nature, our theology would be of a higher strain, and our philosophy no less attractive and veracious. I cannot forget that the Father of Inductive Philosophy was sincerely of the opinion that there were some questions which even science must be content to hand over to religion for their complete, or approximately complete, solution.[1] Science may teach us much, but when we gaze far into the past or far into the future, we must always observe that it signally fails us; we ever find, that between the farthest point to which its deductions may help to lead us, and—the beginning or the end, there is a chasm that cannot be bridged over.

But it is not for me to discuss such things. The main aspect of these sermons is practical and consolatory, not polemical and antagonistic. My humble object has been to put before the young, the generous, and the impressible, some high and ennobling views of Scriptural truth; and if I have succeeded in this great and important object, if I have raised the religious tone of one heart that has gone with my words, if I have been permitted to be the feeble instrument in raising one sinking brother from the deep waters of doubt and perplexity,—if I have pointed out ever so generally to one lone wan-

---

[1] See Bacon, *de Augmentis* iv. 3. Vol. i. p. 605 (ed. Ell.).

derer in this world's weary wilderness the narrow way to Christ, then I shall solemnly rejoice, and my joy no man shall take from me. Then, indeed, I shall feel that I have given up to publicity and criticism my cherished speculations and private convictions, not wholly, not utterly in vain.

To the younger members, then, more especially, of that ancient and illustrious body which I have been appointed to address, I desire earnestly and affectionately to commend these thoughts. There is much in them with which the young will perhaps readily sympathize. There is a speculative tone which is often distasteful to those who are pre-occupied with, what are called, the realities of life, but which rarely fails to interest, and, I most religiously believe, to edify, those on whom the morning sun of life has not yet ceased to shine. To the young, then,—yet not to the young only,—to the generous, the pure, and the thoughtful among us, I humbly dedicate these sermons, with earnest prayer to Almighty God, that His blessing may go with them, and out of their very weakness and imperfection, may perfect His glory and His praise.

ADVERTISEMENT
TO
THE SECOND EDITION.

The present edition, which solely owes its appearance to numerous friendly requests that the Sermons should be reprinted, differs very slightly from the first edition. A few trifling alterations in language have been made here and there, and a few verbal modifications introduced in parts of Sermon V., where the kind criticisms that have been passed on that sermon have shown that such were desirable. A few additions have also been made to the authorities in the notes, but no attempt has been made to alter their general character, it being felt, on mature reflection, that such notes, though only of the slight and unpretending nature alluded to in the Preface, are, perhaps, better adapted to the speculative subjects which they are designed to illustrate, than more elaborate and systematic compilations.

EXETER, *Jan.* 1862.

CONTENTS.

SERMON I.
The Destiny of the Creature.—Vanity 1

SERMON II.
The Destiny of the Creature.—Suffering . 26

SERMON III.
The Destiny of the Creature.—Death 50

SERMON IV.
The Destiny of the Creature.—Restitution 77

SERMON V.
The Threefold Nature of Man . 103

SERMON VI.
The Communion of Saints 126

Notes 147

SERMON I.

THE DESTINY OF THE CREATURE.—VANITY.

Romans viii. 20, 21.

The creature was made subject to vanity, not willingly, but by reason of Him who hath subjected the same, in hope, because the creature itself also shall be delivered from the bondage of corruption into the glorious liberty of the children of God.

THERE are a few texts in the New Testament, more especially in St. Paul's Epistles, that seem to point to the deepest and uttermost secrets of creation. Often half isolated from the argument, emerging suddenly from a more restricted context, gathering up what has seemed specific into declarations most comprehensively general, they reveal to the reader, at one time, such far-reaching issues, at another, such retrospective dispensations, that the immediate occasion, the unfolding argument, or the applied exhortation, seems lost and forgotten in the majesty of the incidental revelation. All we feel conscious of, is seeing along a vista into the past or the future so marvellous yet so divine, that all life seems in an instant to acquire a deeper meaning, all the mystery of our being to assume a fresh significance. The perplexed thoughts of weary years adjust themselves suddenly into order and coherence; the long looked for is at last fully seen; the long searched for at last found.

Of such a class of passages I could not well have chosen a more striking and notable instance than that which will form the subject of our meditations this afternoon. Few texts are more comprehensive; few reach further both into the past and into the future; few afford more serious topics for Christian meditation. I feel, indeed, that in choosing such a text I am, in some degree, laying myself open to the charge of presumption, and of intruding into things not fully revealed; still, in this particular case, I am somewhat emboldened by the remembrance that all the more sober and thoughtful interpreters of the present day are plainly converging to a common explanation of this mysterious passage,[1] and are distinctly tending to re-affirm the ancient and traditional interpretation of the early Church.[2] And again, I cannot be insensible to the fact that our text carries with it practical applications of no common importance,—applications which, by the blessing of the Eternal Spirit, may become fruitful unto salvation, and may serve to add a reality and solemnity to the common aspects of our daily life. These indeed I cannot hope, on the present occasion, to do more than generally indicate; but I feel that

[1] See note A.   [2] See note B.

I am addressing an audience that can readily supply all that may be lacking, and that will perhaps be more benefited by having a few suggestive outlines presented to their view in the compass of a single sermon, than by any attempt to enter into details and enlarge upon applications, which would easily occupy my whole allotted course. I trust, indeed, with the blessing of God, hereafter to discuss kindred and illustrative subjects; but this, on which we are now about to dwell—the subjection of the creature to vanity—will, I am sure, be most beneficially treated, if reduced to the limits of one sermon, and exhibited at one view in all its characteristic unity and comprehensiveness.

Before entering more immediately upon the consideration of the separate clauses, let me call your attention to two facts in reference to our present text: *First*,—that few passages have tended more distinctly to call out the exegetical or doctrinal peculiarities of successive expositors, and consequently, that few passages require us more cautiously to exclude all interpretations that have a subjective aspect, and reflect too strongly the prevailing sentiments and opinions of the age in which they appeared. *Secondly*,—that no text has suffered more from the arbitrary limitation of the terms in which it is expressed; and that in no case will it be found more advisable to give boldly to every term the most comprehensive meaning the context will warrant, and to every clause its fullest and most extended significance.

The application of these two considerations meets us in the first clause: 'The creature was made subject to vanity.' On the latitude assigned to the term 'creature,' or, as it may perhaps be better translated 'creation,' the interpretation of the passage mainly depends. And here, without occupying your time with detailed reasons, I will venture to assert, that, after most anxious consideration, I cannot doubt that Irenæus and the Greek Fathers were right in giving the term 'creation' its widest application,[1] and in referring it to all creation, animate and inanimate, which stands in any degree of relation to man. I am aware that the great name of Augustine is urged as confining the term to mankind in their unconverted state; but if you examine the passage where this opinion is maintained,[2] you will at once see how clearly his own words show, that he here receded from his usual expansive interpretation of Scripture under the pressure of Manichæan antagonism. I am aware, too, that arguments have been founded on the impropriety of ascribing a feeling of yearning and longing to an inanimate world: these, however, we may be content to pass over in silence, when biblical language supplies so many illustrations, and when the most calm and unimpassioned thinkers have felt no difficulty in using words and expressions in a great degree similar and analogous.[3]

---

[1] See note C.   [2] See note D.   [3] See note E.

Without pausing longer on this point, let us at once pass onward to the mournful declaration that is embodied in the first clause,—'The creation was made subject to vanity.' Who can resist pausing on so startling a revelation? Who, as he turns his eyes on the wide realms of creation, does not feel strange queries forcing themselves on his attention, and demanding of him an answer? Who, as he gazes on the fairer features of nature, the sunny landscape, the sheltering woods, the clustered mountains, does not feel the force of the inscrutable antithesis? All so fair, yet all subject to such a destiny; so beautiful, yet so doomed. Is there one graver thinker among us who has not craved for the solution of a mystery so seemingly inexplicable? 'What!' we sometimes say, in our deep perplexity, 'what can be the meaning of this law of vanity in reference to creation generally? I can understand the ruin of my own soul, I am forced to acknowledge its corrupting lusts, I can feel its rending passions, I can trace out the slow corrosion of evil habits, the convulsive movements of sudden sins,—I can mark all this in myself and others; but these guiltless creatures of God's hand, what have *they* done? These animals that minister to my wants, and die unrecked of and unheeded, whence come their strange accumulations of sufferings? This wide-spread plant-world, that contributes to my food, or bears balm to my wounds, whence comes its often thwarted development and stinted growth, its palpable subjection to something more than perishableness, its bondage to something worse than decay? Is there no answer? Is the attribute of Preserver to be denied to the Creator, or given only under such limitations as make it a very mockery and a bitterness. Verily, is there no answer?'

Yes, surely, the text supplies an answer,—deep and mournful, yet, if rightly understood, unspeakably consolatory. The answer is, that it was 'by reason of Him who subjected it.' Not, observe, by Him, simply and directly, but, *by reason of Him*,[1] owing to some determination of His counsels, some interposition of His will. And who was *He?* Are we to say with some interpreters, that it was Adam, and refer to a mere man what seems to involve the agency and providence of God? Are we to say that it was Satan, and introduce conceptions of a destroyer and an adversary in the consideration of a text, which tells alone of the sovereign will of a Creator and Restorer?[2] Can we consistently believe it to be other than God,—God the all-wise and all-just, who was moved to subject His creation to this mournful law; who, in accordance with the deep harmony that exists between all parts of His creation, was pleased to decree that, along the cloudy paths of suffering and mutability, all things should emerge together into the perfect day.

But who that has deeply considered this subject

---

[1] διὰ τὸν ὑποτάξαντα: comp. Winer, *Gr.* § 49. c, p. 356, note.
[2] See note F.

would not fain ask still further, *What is the exact nature of this subjection*, and, above all, *when did it take place?* Is it coeval with the first dawn of creation, or is it to be referred to an historic era no older than the race to which we belong? These are momentous questions, which no sound interpretation of this text must leave wholly unanswered. With regard to the first, let us be especially careful to bear in mind the peculiar amplitude of the term 'vanity.' It is not said that the creation was subject to death or corruption, though both lie involved in the expression, but to something more frightfully generic, to something almost worse than non-existence,—to purposelessness, to an inability to realize its natural tendencies and the ends for which it was called into being, to baffled endeavour and mocked expectation, to a blossoming and not bearing fruit, a pursuing and not attaining, yea, and as the analogies of the language of the original significantly imply,—to a searching, and never finding.[1]

Let us bear this well in mind, lest we find ourselves involved in those difficulties into which nearly all have fallen, who have sought to limit this purely scriptural, but profoundly significant and comprehensive term.

But further, *When did this subjection take place?* Is it, as some of the popular thinkers of our own day would fain persuade us, in consequence of some primal

[1] See note G.

law, that reaches backward into the furthest regions of the past, and that was originally designed to include both us and all mankind in the necessities of a common bondage?[1] Or, is it not rather,—as, indeed, our own hearts already half tell us, and the guarded language of our present text seems not obscurely to indicate,—not the original law, but a counter-law, a judicial dispensation, which opposition to the will of a beneficent Creator served to call forth and to ratify. In one word, is it not *sin* that has caused all this, that has cast this shade on creation, and drawn the bar sinister across the broad shield of the handiwork of God? It must be so. And yet it is a plausible hypothesis that refers all to a primal law impressed on the earliest manifestations of creation. It is a startling retrospect that shows us imperfection and incompleteness in the first commencement of being, and discloses to our view evidences of sufferings and death in the most remote periods of the earth's history. Does not science seem to contribute to the decision? Do not the very stones we tread on show to us the hooked tooth, the beak for rending, and the claw for tearing? Do not the rocks tell of rapine and destruction and death, ages before man was called into existence?[2] Does it not seem, then, that, after all, we must rectify our conceptions, and refer this subjection to some law which existed long anterior to man, to which man must have yielded whether he had sinned or no, and to which his actual

---

[1] See note II. [2] See note I.

sin only added some embitterment and enhancement? So a popular philosophy would suggest. But, independently of the strong feeling of our hearts,—independently of the connexion of sin and death, which the verses preceding the text distinctly imply, independently of the reference, in the verses that follow, to the bond that unites the future of man with the future of all the other portions of creation with which he stands in any degree in contact,—independently of the strong presumption, that is thus suggested, of some melancholy past, in which both were united,—independently of all these considerations, can we say that such an hypothesis is in any way compatible with the plain declarations of the text, or with the simplest deductions which are suggested by the analogy of Scripture? Does it not fail in several important particulars?

In the first place, does it not tacitly confound the more generic term *vanity* with the more specific term *death?* In the second place, does it not assume this most unlikely fact, that man, created as he was in the image of his Maker, and framed as he was by the special operation of His divine hands, was to share the lot of creatures called into being under conditions significantly different; not separately formed, but collectively summoned forth from the secret chambers of a prolific earth? Is it not, further, almost at variance with the cardinal text, 'Death passed through unto all men;'¹ not *all*

---

¹ Rom. v. 12, εἰς πάντας ἀνθρώπους διῆλθεν.

things but *all men*, as if it were almost intended to mark, that death was a law and a process that originally had no existence or significance for man? And lastly, does it not rob of all its real meaning and potency the curse which man's sin brought on the material earth, and by consequence, on all the forms of life to which that earth gave origin: 'And to Adam He said, cursed is the ground for thy sake; in sorrow shalt thou eat of it all the days of thy life; thorns also and thistles it shall bring forth to thee; and thou shalt eat the herb of the field.'[1]

Are the theories of a speculative philosophy to lead us implicitly to deny such mighty and such specific declarations? God forbid!

I do not doubt then, brethren, that the counter-law, by which the whole creation has been made subject to vanity, is to be referred to no other epoch than the fall of man. Prior to that time all nature was lovingly obeying the laws impressed on it by God; the herb was yielding its seed, the animal was bringing forth its kind, each to be succeeded by a more numerous growth of its own species, or to make way for more highly organized types of animal or vegetable life. Decay meant reproduction, dissolution development, death a return into the general life of nature, which was to be succeeded by a more prolific emergence. All was obeying the beneficent laws of the Creator; everything was tending in its

---

[1] Gen. iii. 17.

own measure and degree, to a final perfection, and—if the speculation be not over bold—to a final annihilation of any evil that might have flowed as a consequence from the fall of angels, by those very fore-ordered processes to which we, in our ignorance, give the names of incompleteness and imperfection.

While all things were thus harmoniously fulfilling the law of their existence, while everything was thus stretching forwards to higher measures of perfection, Man, the highest and noblest of God's creatures, formed out of the elements of the same material world,—yet with the image of his Maker on his brow, and the breath of divine life in his nostrils,—was called on the theatre of Being to lead all things onwards to their highest developments, to act the part of the choragus of creation, and, himself exempted from death and dissolution, to assist throughout the whole development of the mighty working, whereby God was to become all in all.

Pause only, brethren, and consider the mystical relation of man to his Creator, and to that earth from which he was taken. Mark how in that wondrous union of body, soul, and spirit,[1] man was fitted by his Maker to be a kind of mediator between the Infinite Father and the finite, but blameless creatures of His hand. Consider only, how the body of man is the link between the material world and the im-

---

[1] On this subject see Sermon V.

material soul; and how the soul is the bond between the body and the spirit; and how the spirit is that which formed some medium of connexion between the soul of man—the true centre of his personality—and the eternal and infinite Spirit of God.

When a being thus constituted, thus mysteriously related to the material world, fell from his allegiance to his Creator, can we readily believe that creation was a mere uninterested spectator? Does not every consideration prepare us for what we know from other passages of Scripture, and which our present text seems clearly to confirm,—that man's voluntary sin produced an effect upon the whole material world; that it cast its shade over all the realms of nature, and caused creation, involuntarily and reluctantly (what a mournful and suggestive antithesis there lies in those words, 'not willing'), to submit itself to the effect of an act committed with the full assent of a rational will, and on the deliberate choice of a voluntary agent? Yes, let us doubt not that the sin of man wrought all the ruin that we now can trace both in nature and ourselves, and caused the beneficent Creator, in conformity with those counsels sealed in silence from the beginning of the world, to subject all that, of which man was the pre-eminent creation, to purposelessness, vanity, and corruption.

Is there in such a dispensation anything so totally inconceivable, so wholly at variance with the analogies of things as to make us doubt the possibility of its existence, or to preclude our believing that sin is an interposing cloud between us and the Father of Lights, that has cast its palpable shadow on the face of all created things,—that the world since the fall is, as it were, *a world without sunshine?* To adopt an illustration from the ordinary appearances of nature; what a difference there is between the aspects of a fair landscape when viewed under a clouded, and under an unclouded sky! What a real difference, not in sentiment and feeling, but in actual appearance, between the darkening mountain, the misty valley, the obliterated distance, and the joyance and beauty of the same scene when gladdened with sunshine! How shadow enhances substance, how form becomes defined and distance expanded, how each individual object seems subordinated to the general effect, and how the whole scene seems only to suggest continuance and extension, and to be itself only a part of a yet fairer and more radiant distance! Even so is it now. We cannot, indeed, fully verify the simile; we know not what the world actually *was*, still we can form some inferences by observing what it *is*. Everywhere the same appearance of something that be-clouds and darkens, everywhere the same traces of aberration from appointed ends, the same hints of perverted tendencies, the same tokens of frustration and decay. Even with the acknowledged phenomena of rapine and death in a pre-Adamite world, borne steadily in view and made the most of in argument, set now before your eyes the scarcely doubtful instances of depravation of instincts, the exhibitions of wanton cruelty in the lower animals, the occasional glimpses of something worse than ferocity, the traces of a startling malignity, especially in some of the species of more venomous reptiles, which it seems hard indeed to believe was natural and original. Add all these things together, and then finally consider if there be anything really inconceivable in the thought, that the effects of man's sin are to be traced in the material world, yea, that the whole creation has become subject to vanity owing to the rebellion of its suzerain, and is now, as the Apostle tells us, ever groaning and travailing in its alien and unnatural bondage.

But is it to last for ever? No verily! The most consolatory, though most mysterious portion of the text now claims our attention. This subjection on which we have been meditating was mitigated by the infusion of a hope, which remains to this day unchanged and unimpaired. 'The creation was subjected to vanity,' says the Apostle, ' in hope *that* itself, the creation (for this, I cannot doubt, is the most simple and natural translation of the clause)[1]—the seemingly hopeless creation—shall be delivered from the bondage of corruption into the glorious liberty of the children of God.' In these consolatory words the point of real and startling importance is the close bond that connects man with the material world, especially

---

[1] See note J.

in the relation of *time*. With man's sin came at once the curse that fell upon the earth; thorn and thistle began to germinate the very day that Adam sinned; confusion and discord began at once to work amid the tendencies of created things. And even so shall it be in the restitution. The earnest expectation of the creature waits for no doubtful or chimerical future, for no ill-defined or uncertain hour of emancipation; it waits, as the Spirit of God here infallibly declares, for no less a sure and certain epoch than that of the manifestation of the sons of God. The restoration of man and the world will be as contemporaneous as their first bondage and subjection. When the number of the elect is complete, when the last of the mystical one hundred and forty and four thousand[1] shall receive the seal of God on his forehead, when the last drop shall be added to the brimming cup of the afflictions of Christ,[2] the last tear shed, the last sigh breathed into the air, the glorification of the creature will have fully commenced, the sunlight of the unclouded presence of God will again irradiate His works, the weary night of creation will at length have passed, the long-looked-for dawn at last come. And now all are longing and all are tarrying; bound together by the affinities of a common spiritual principle; united in ruin, yet still united in hope. While faith, in the form of belief to the Christian, and dim intuitions to the heathen, is the prerogative of the

---

[1] Rev. vii. 4.   [2] See Sermon II. p. 42.

rational creature, *hope* is the gift that has not been denied to the irrational creation. Hope is common to all: hope binds nature and mankind in a close and enduring union. And so now all are waiting. The Church is waiting; the souls under the altar are waiting;[1] the kindreds of the earth are waiting; the world of animate things is waiting; the whole realm of inanimate nature is waiting; yea, more, as the next verse discloses, waiting in self-acknowledged suffering, groaning and travailing as in birth-pains, conscious of a common captivity and a common ruin. Not only we ourselves, the Apostle tells us, the rational and accountable creatures of God's hand,—not only we, that smaller company who have the first fruits of the Spirit, groan within ourselves,[2] struggling for freedom from vanity and corruption,—not only we, the chosen ones, are thus longing and travailing, but with us all creation is blended in that never-quenched aspiration. All the sufferings of the wide-spread domains of nature form a part of that earnest and mournful cry.

All that *animals* suffer at the hands of man,—all that they suffer from one another, all their exhibitions of wanton cruelty, their deep-seated aversions and connatural hostilities;—all, again, that *nature* suffers from the hand of man, the poisoned vegetation round peopled cities, the blazing prairie, the desolated forest,[3] —all that it suffers from the wildness or churlishness

---

[1] Rev. vi. 9.   [2] Rom. viii. 23.   [3] See note K.

of the elements, the storm-swept champaign, the inundated valley, the convulsed landscape,—all that tells of frustrated growth and retarded progress, untimely violence and freakish change,—all tend to swell that mighty cry of suffering and travail that is now ever sounding in the ears of God,—all serve to call forth the deep longing for the hour when man, the masterpiece of God's works, shall be clothed with incorruption, when nature shall be restored, and the apocalyptic vision of the Apostle shall be a mighty and living reality. 'And I saw a new heaven and a new earth, for the first heaven and the first earth were passed away, and there was no more sea.'[1]

And now, to gather up our foregoing meditations into a few distinct statements, it would seem that the investigation of this profound text leads us to the following result.

First, the recognition of primal laws mysteriously wise and mysteriously beneficent, of which the characteristics were, providential development and conservative change,—laws that might *possibly* have involved some reference to the lapse in a spirit-world,[2] but in which there was no trace of perverted action, confusion, or vanity.

Secondly, that man, by an act of disobedience, brought himself and his race under the alien dominion of suffering and death, and caused all the rest of creation to be subject to a counter-law of

[1] Rev. xxi. 1. [2] See Sermon II. p. 29.

vanity, depraved instincts, perverted tendencies, and injurious change.

Thirdly, that this subjection was, nevertheless, mercifully alleviated,—to man, by the blessings of a sure promise,—to the other portions of nature by the infusion of a hope; and that both thus bound together in one common feeling of longing and expectancy, are awaiting that redemption of the body in man which shall be the immediate precursor of the restitution of the world and the consummation of all things in Christ.

Such, brethren, are the principal features of a text that has not inappropriately been termed 'the Evangel of creation;' such, a few leading outlines of one of the most comprehensive revelations in the Book of Life.

In a subject so elevated, involving so many and such mighty issues, and opening up so many avenues of speculation, I dare not hope to have done more than to have secured a partial or suspended assent: yet if to one of you, my elder brethren, these fleeting words have tended to supply an answer to one single doubt that may have tried your spirits,—if in you, my younger brethren, the general subject has awakened any higher aspirations, or aroused you to a truer consciousness of the deep mystery of life, I shall solemnly rejoice, and shall offer up my prayer to Almighty God that He may quicken us all to look forward with more longing eyes and more ready hearts to the coming of our Lord. May He make us feel more vividly the power of His resurrection working in our souls, and trace with holy awe, both in ourselves and all things around us, the development of the mighty counsels of redeeming grace and restoring love.

Let me conclude with two out of the many practical reflections, which this present subject seems most especially calculated to awaken.

First, let us not fail to recognise the disclosure that is here made of the frightful nature of sin, considered as something spreading and diffusive. If, on the one hand, the intense nature of sin, its blackness and venom,—in a word, its nature in reference to *uality*, finds its fullest exponent in the awful truths that the Son of the ever-living God emptied Himself of His glories to redeem fallen man;—so, on the other hand, the diffusive nature of sin,—its nature viewed in reference to *quantity*, is nowhere more strikingly disclosed than in the revelation that is now before us. Does not our text imply that sin was such that it spread over a whole creation, marred the harmonies of a world, pervaded the substance and the produce of a fruitful earth, entered into all the varied realms of animal life,—calling out antipathies, multiplying sufferings, and giving a new and bitter aspect to beneficent laws of transmutation and change?

And yet how lightly we talk of sin! How readily we lend an ear to any one who teaches us to think hopefully of this spreading ulcer, that is eating away the very heart and life of us and of all things! The forward thinkers, as they are termed, of our own age are ever too ready to persuade us that sin, after all, is only something isolated and external, merely an immoral atmosphere that always remains both in quantity and quality the same. But is it so? Can we dare, with such a text before us as that on which we have been meditating, cheat ourselves with such hopeless sophistries? Surely, if there is one truth more than another which our present text tends to enforce and to enhance, it is this, that sin is co-extensive with every development of the animate and inanimate world,—that it is the noxious bindweed which is winding itself round every form of a once fair creation, ever blossoming into vanity and suffering, ever ripening into the fruitage of death and corruption.

But *secondly*, let us turn to the consolatory reflection, that though the old creation is thus marred and ruined, yet that the new creation has already begun. Yea, doubtless it has already begun. It was ratified on our Master's cross. It was commenced in His resurrection. It has become developed by baptism in His name; His Church is its first fruits; His grace its moving principle; His love the mystery of its evolution. And that love is pervading all things, yea, why should we fear to say it, not only the inward and spiritual, but the outward and material world. Though we may not be able to distinctly recognise all its plastic powers,—though fools may mock, and gainsayers deny,—though moralists may tell us that amelioration is a dream, and progress a mere motion in a circle,—though we ourselves may at times doubt our own hopes,—yet if we have eyes to see and hearts to believe, we may still feel some present loosening of the chain that binds all things to the law of vanity and corruption. We may trace alleviations of suffering in many things around us, often in strange and unlooked-for ways; sometimes by incidental discoveries, sometimes by more deliberate applications of the great laws of nature, those so-called mechanical triumphs of which our age is so fondly yet so ignorantly proud. There are commencements everywhere. Though we may not see more than mere beginnings and initial movements, though our eyes may fall on sleep before the lights of the coming day have appeared above the still clouded horizon, yet in patience and hope let us possess our souls; let us quit ourselves like men in the hourly struggle with sin, and remember that every triumph over a temptation in our Redeemer's name, every victory over a warring lust in the power of the Spirit, is an unwinding of a chain of the bondage of vanity, is an act in the emancipation of a world.

With such high thoughts as these, with such a lofty destiny before us, can we remain insensible to the solemn and vital call to practical holiness which these meditations cannot fail to supply? Shall we, my elder brethren, inmates of this ancient seat of learning and piety, we to whom God has vouchsafed so large a measure of His grace, forget our high calling of teaching and guiding others, and merge ourselves in apathy and selfishness? Is it for such as us to spend the best days of our lives in dreamy or perverted hopes, to think that this earth is for mere intellectual triumphs and self-glorifying progress, when all around is suffering and travail? Shall we be narrow and churlish in our love, when everything so tends to call it forth? With such a struggle going on around us, are we to shut ourselves up in our little citadels of fancied pre-eminence, or worse, with a petty spirit of detraction, with unkindly words or mordant satire, to disown our fraternal bond, and imitate the very antipathies of a lower and captive creation? Are we to become daily more unfruitful in our faith, and to think that calm abstractions will lead us to heaven, and a decent apathy avail us in an hour, when nought save the energy of vital belief either can or will fit us to be the co-operators with our redeeming and restoring Lord?

Or again, is it for you, my younger brethren, to dally with sin and corruption in its coarser and more repulsive forms, when the suffering voice of nature is telling you how the iron of bondage is entering into its very soul, and is calling upon you in the strength and glory of youth and life, to devote the blessed gifts of a fresh and buoyant heart to the service of the Almighty Restorer? Can you resist the summons to join the armies of heaven in their holy war against sin and death, and to be found the loyal and true-hearted skirmishers before the mighty host that is mustering and gathering, unfolding its banners and marshalling its legions, momently awaiting the κέλευσμα,[1] the signal-shout, when He that hath on His thigh and His vesture a name written—King of Kings and Lord of Lords[2]—shall go forth conquering and to conquer?

In one word, the summary and great practical lesson of all that I have said, is the necessity of personal and individual holiness. Man's sin, yea, one man's sin, cast all this shadow on creation; man's holiness, the holiness of the many, shall co-operate in its restoration. All things join in this call to practical holiness, and shall it remain for ever unnoticed and unheeded? God our Creator calls on us to be holy; He has called us, as He himself says by the mouth of His Apostle, not to selfishness, not to uncleanness, but to holiness.[3] God our Redeemer calls on us to follow the steps of His pure and holy life. God the Sanctifier pleads with our hearts, and with groans that tongue cannot tell, calls on us to fulfil our Maker's will—His will, even our sanctification.[4] Our suffering brethren call upon us. Yea, and all Nature mutely joins in that never-ceasing appeal: the animals that gaze strangely and wistfully in our

---

[1] 1 Thess. v. 16.   [2] Rev. xix. 16.   [3] 1 Thess. iv. 7.
[4] 1 Thess. iv. 3.

faces; the short-lived and fading loveliness of all things around us,—all are calling on us, consciously or unconsciously, not to put back the hour of their restitution, not to delay the coming of the glorious liberty of the sons of God. And can we resist such calls? Shall we individually contribute nothing to such mighty issues, or, worse still, shall we arrest the progress that has already been made? Already new and mysterious forces are at work all around us, silently permeating all forms of life, secretly entering into all elements of the material world. Let us bethink ourselves of our responsibility if we now join with sin and corruption. Let us pray to remember in the hour of temptation that to yield is not only to commit an individual act against our own souls, but to join a triple league that we renounced in baptism, to go over to the adversary, and, as far as in us lies, to arrest the development of the new creation, to rivet the bondage of corruption,—nay, more, to be found fighters against a reconciling and restoring God.

From such frightful antagonisms,—from such semblances of the malice of an apostate creation, may He, in the largeness of His mercies, ever turn us and protect us. May He call us, and may we hear. May every soul among us be moved to do his part in a world's restoration; that so, when the great Restorer's feet shall stand on Olivet, in that mystic day 'when it shall be neither clear nor dark, but in the evening time it shall be light,"[1] we may be numbered with His faithful ones who have borne the heat and burden of the day,— and to whom there remaineth rest for evermore.

---

[1] Zechah. xiv. 4.

SERMON II.

THE DESTINY OF THE CREATURE.—SUFFERING.

JOB xiv. 1.

Man that is born of a woman is of few days, and full of trouble.

IN our meditations last Sunday, brethren, we were led, by the solemn tenor of the profound text which I attempted to illustrate, to sad and serious views on the present condition of the creature. We were brought to acknowledge in all that creation with which we have any direct connexion, the working of a mysterious and pervasive counter-law; we were led to contemplate a destiny—if I may use such a term—of all created things around us, startling in its universality, mournful in its evolution, and strikingly suggestive in respect of its origin and early development. Though we were obliged to pass over much that in detail was inexplicable or insoluble,—though there were suggested to us many questions, to which we could only give faltering, and perhaps unsatisfying answers, we did, I trust, still distinctly perceive and acknowledge the existence of laws of perverted action, depravations of instincts, thwarted developments, injurious change,—all of which, under the generic term of Vanity, were to be referred for their origin to the disobedience and fall of man. We may now suitably and profitably take a step onward. We have contemplated the universal subjection: let us now proceed to trace out its more concentrated and specific manifestations in the mystery of *suffering*, and so prepare ourselves for a future consideration of its more complete development in the awful climax of *death*.

Yet let us be careful to order our thoughts soberly and wisely. Let us attempt no comprehensive estimate of the various forms and degrees of suffering, but simply, by the light of Scripture alone, endeavour to gain a clear view of the aspects in which it is presented to us both in the Old and in the New Testament. Let us mark the changed relations it assumes, the altered attitudes in which it is found in the two Dispensations,—and then from all, let us, by the help of God, draw such practical consolations as may serve to make us more bravely patient, more hopeful, yea, more thankful, in our sojourn in a world which at every turn flings back on us the shadows of our own disobedience.

It is clear that such a mode of treating this difficult subject tends inevitably to limit our meditation to suffering, as seen and felt in our own race. But it must be so. For the origin and import of suffering, considered in its most comprehensive relations, and regarded as the lot of other orders of creation beside our own, involves mysteries, and apparently points backward to primal dispensations, which on this side the grave we can never hope to understand, and on which it is fruitless, if not irreverent, to speculate. It *is* certainly, and it must be acknowledged a startling fact, that ages before the sin of man cast the shadow of vanity on the world, suffering in one of its forms, the corporeal, was certainly present. As I said last Sunday, the very stones and rocks bear witness of it; the acknowledged presence in the pre-Adamite world of the fierce and fell race of the carnivorous animals,[1] renders its past existence a certainty; and to deny it is as fruitless as to deny its present manifestations and potency. We must distinctly admit it as a startling fact,—a fact of which we cannot venture to give any explanation, but still a fact which need cause us to feel no practical difficulties, and which is in no way incompatible with our conceptions of God as a just and beneficent governor of the world. Though attempts to explain the seeming difficulty are worse than idle, yet let me offer briefly the two following observations:—*First*, in every endeavour to view suffering in its most comprehensive and general aspects, we must be especially careful to draw a clear line of demarcation between the corporeal sufferings of the individuals that belong to lower genera unendued with foresight and reason, and the mixed *mental* and corporeal

---

See note A.

sufferings of a personal and intelligent being, the immediate child and offspring of God. Between the individuals of races, brought forth by a prolific earth,[1] and the living soul that drew its existence from the breath of God, the difference is really so great that it does not seem either unreasonable or evasive to pause before we refer to a common origin, or group in common analogies, the sufferings of two orders of creation thus widely different in origin, relations, and characteristics. *Secondly*, the scattered hints and speculations of earlier writers, afterwards more fully developed by some of the deeper thinkers of the seventeenth century, that regard the early history of the world and the fall of angels as in *some sort* of connexion, are certainly not wholly unworthy of our consideration.[2] How far the disturbance caused by that fearful lapse was propagated through the other realms of creation we know not. How far demoniacal malignity might have been permitted to introduce or multiply sufferings in the early animal world, Scripture does not even incidentally reveal. Still, it does not seem utterly presumptuous to imagine that there might have been the same powers of evil partially and permissively at work in a pre-Adamite world, that at a later period, when man's sin had wrought a still more frightful confusion, were permitted to drive the swine down the steeps of Gennesareth.[3]

---

[1] Gen. i. 24.   [2] See note B.   [3] Matth. viii. 32.

To which let us add by way of corollary, that if we are here thought to open ourselves to the objection of modern speculation—viz., that even thus, under such permissive aspects, we are ascribing evil to God as its remoter origin, we still shrink not from the pressure of such an inference. Let us remember that the Lord has declared twice by the mouths of His greatest prophets, with all imaginable distinctness, that he is the Creator of evil as well as of good[1]—yes, unrestrictedly the Creator of it; and that it is the eternal prerogative of His omnipotence that out of the mouth of the Most High should proceed both the one and the other.[2] Let us only be prepared to view the indissoluble connexion of evil, suffering, and sin, and then whether the supposed evil we contemplate be Adamite or pre-Adamite, mundane or ante-mundane, we need fear no Manichæan sophistries, we need seek to shelter ourselves under no spurious views of the Divine benevolence.

All, however, we can safely say is this,—that man's sin caused all things to be subjected to vanity; and that one of the outcomings of this vanity was suffering and death to the race of man, embitterment and enhancement of suffering to the races of the animal creation,[3]—a signal embitterment, if we take nothing further into account than the accumulation of it, which is to be referred to the tyranny, the cruelty, and the perverted wants of the fallen race of mankind.

---

[1] Isaiah xlv. 7.   [2] Lam. iii. 38.   [3] See note C.

But let us leave these difficult questions, and now address ourselves solely to the aspects and significance of *human* suffering as respectively exhibited by the two Testaments. The contrasts are very striking, instructive, and consolatory.

To begin with the Old Testament; the first thing that cannot fail to strike us is the melancholy and gloomy aspect in which suffering is nearly always presented to our view. It seems ever to reflect the just wrath of Jehovah, ever to be designed as something punitive and judicial. We recognise it distinctly in the first sentence on sin; we hear it in the language addressed to the first mortal sinners; 'And unto the woman He said, I will greatly multiply thy sorrow and conception,'[1]—' and unto Adam He said, cursed is the ground for thy sake, in sorrow shalt thou eat of it all the days of thy life.'[2] We trace it in the deepening curse on Cain, in which, beyond all the suffering of ill-requited labour and toil, there appear the more peculiarly mental sufferings of exile from a home of love, the dreary lot of the fugitive and the vagabond.[3] We see it further in all the histories of the patriarchs, with whom sorrow and suffering, if not always viewed as the immediate result of sin, were still recognised as belonging to the inevitable condition of sinful mortality: 'Few and evil have been the days of my years.'[4] We

---

[1] Gen. iii. 16.   [2] Gen. iii. 17.   [3] Gen. iv. 12.
[4] Comp. Gen. xlvii. 9.

may trace it onward through the whole of the sacred volume, and whether in the language of history, meditation, or prophecy, we still perceive the same dreary aspects of suffering, the same dark background of sin, the same cheerless recognition of an universal lot, the same sense of chastised disobedience. Group together all the more distinct notices of suffering in the Old Testament, and they will ever be found to reflect or to imply one of two things; either a distinct connexion with sin, more especially in its aspect of disobedience; or, on the other hand, the recognition of a common lot, *in mundo pressuram*, unalterable and inevitable, untempered and unrelieved. Of the first, a striking verification will be found in the curses from Ebal,[1] and the still more frightful denunciations of the 26th chapter of Leviticus,[2]—in which every form of mortal misery, mental and corporeal, written and unwritten, is declared as the certain sequel of disobedience, with an appalling exactness and circumstantiality. Of the second, we nowhere find a sadder outpouring than in the words of our text, which, with such a melancholy significance, point backward to its origin, and to the mediate fountain of all its bitter waters. 'Man that is born of a woman has but a short time to live and is full of misery.'

We deny not, indeed, that in the Old Dispensation many of God's chosen servants were permitted,

---

[1] Deut. xxviii. 15. [2] Ver. 14. sq.

by the gladdening light of Messianic prophecies, to enjoy glimpses of a future when the tears should be wiped away from all eyes,[1]—glimpses of a future that made the present seem more light and endurable. This the author of the Epistle to the Hebrews[2] forbids us to doubt; this the great cloud of witnesses will not permit us to disbelieve. Abraham that looked for the city that has foundations,—Sarah that judged Him faithful that had promised,—Moses that esteemed the reproach of Christ greater riches than the treasures in Egypt, and endured as seeing Him that is invisible,—all remind us that in every age there were thousands to whom suffering must have worn aspects that were not always clouded with the gloom of retrospect. Still the light was ever ready to fade, the gloom to deepen. The promise seemed far off, the future distant, and perhaps unrealizable. Nothing appeared really sure and palpable save the weary present, and the unalterable past,—the lost paradise,—the cursed earth,—the doomed race,—the heritage of sin,—the lineage of corruption. On this side a painful and joyless birth, on that side Sheol with its sad imagery of forgetfulness and darkness,[3] —a darkness broken by but a few rays of quickening light; and between, a melancholy interspace of life, so bemocked by vanity and beclouded with suffering, that the deep thinker of the early dispensation must often have lost sight of the very prerogatives of his

---

[1] Isaiah xxv. 8.   [2] Ch. xi. 2, sq.   [3] See Note D.

own humanity, and have cried out in his bitterness with the old world's wisest man, 'Man hath no pre-eminence above a beast; for all is vanity. All go unto one place. All are of the dust, and all turn to dust again.'[1]

We deny not again that several instances may be collected, especially from the Psalms, in which the more peculiarly evangelical aspects of suffering—its purifying and emendatory characteristics—are distinctly to be recognised. Still, even in these, the accurate reader will rarely fail to discover in the context some reference, more or less distinct, to the judicial nature of suffering, or to the immutable principles of divine government,—the awful justice of God, that faithfulness, that trueness to His own nature and decrees, which the Psalmist failed not to ascribe to His Creator, even when, in His afflictive dispensations, he was enabled to recognise the outlines of a teaching of mercy, 'It is good for me that I have been afflicted,—*that I might learn thy statutes.*'[2] Nay, more, it does not seem too much to say that the specifically Christian idea of suffering,—as probationary, purifying, or emendatory, seems not to have found an expression in any definite word in the language of the Old Covenant. Nearly every word that presents to us the idea of suffering, trouble, or affliction, has some philological affinity to ideas of burden, pressure, fall, ruin, snare, hostility, terror,

---

[1] Eccles. iii. 19, 20.   [2] Psalm cxix. 71.

destruction: more than one term blends cause and effect, and exhibits the ideas of affliction and sin in closest union; while, philologically considered, the most elevated conception of human suffering does not appear to rise beyond that of bearing injuries rather than of returning them.[1] So indelible does this impress seem on the very language of the Old Testament, that the familiar πάθημα of the New Testament, with its implied ideas of endurance and grief,[2] finds no place in the Greek translation of the Old Testament, just as 'suffering' does not, I believe, occur anywhere in our own English Version.

Such things can scarcely be accidental; such hints can hardly be wholly without significance. Such observations on the letter combine singularly with our meditations on the spirit of the Old Covenant, and seem to tell us, that in all its representations of human suffering, it bears, both within and without, a startling testimony to its original nature and significance,—chastised disobedience and penal sorrow.

But were the aspects of suffering ever to remain unchanged? Was the burden of the curses of Ebal ever to be felt in every afflictive dispensation? Was sorrow only to recall with all retrospective bitterness, sin, and disobedience? Ah, no! when God and man were reconciled, when the eternal Son became

---

[1] See note E. [2] See note F.

man, and shared all man's sufferings, then indeed all was changed: every feebler discord was lost in the universal harmony. Death became life, and sorrow joy, and vanity hope, and suffering—suffering, that bitter evidence of sin, that embodiment of a primal curse, became a very precursor of salvation, a token of a Father's love, a state that received the Saviour's blessing, yea, strange and almost awful to say, an enduring bond of union between us and our God. On this mighty change let us spend our remaining thoughts. Let us now turn to the New Covenant, and endeavour humbly and thankfully to estimate the changed aspects in which suffering is exhibited, and, by the help of a few cardinal and consolatory passages, to behold the mystery of its final issues and development.

In the Old Testament we have just seen that suffering appears mainly under one of two aspects; either as the punishment of disobedience, or as the evidence of a common lot, and the token of a common fall. It was in fact essentially *retrospective ;* its looks were ever turned backwards to the circumstances of its first origin, and to the early issues of primal transgression. Its characteristic was retrospect. But in the New Testament all is reversed. There suffering is essentially *prospective ;*—prospective, as turning the inward eye towards Him, who, after hallowing suffering by taking its uttermost measures on Himself, is now sitting at the right hand of God, the helper of the labouring and the refresher of the weary;—prospective, as teaching us to gaze ever more and more longingly to the city that has foundations, and to the rest that remaineth for the children of God.

Prospective is it, as turning the sufferer's eye to his once suffering but now glorified Lord. For who that has really suffered has not felt that in gazing upward toward the Prince of sufferers, all things become changed in their relations? The melancholy past merges into the present, and the present becomes lost in a future,—a future of hope, a future of mercy, a future that swallows up all sorrows, stills the cry of all anguish, deadens the edge of all pain. There with Him is all that we have lost, and all that we have mourned for; there the loved ones that have gone before; there the innocent joys of childhood that soon fleeted by; there the quick sympathies that soon were checked; there the warm affections that soon grew cold; there the fair hopes to which disappointment brought blight and decay. All are with Him. And to Him,—if our hearts yet remain true to God and to our better selves, every suffering only tends to bring us nearer and nearer. We gaze only the more earnestly there, where we know we shall find all : ' Where our treasure is, there shall our heart be also.'[1]

Prospective also is suffering as teaching us to look for the final rest. It was this prospective element

---

[1] Matth. vi. 21.

that taught the feeble to glory amid their tribulations, and the weak to be strong. Yea, further, this has sustained those who have entered into the more mystic realm of mental and spiritual suffering. This has bound up hearts that have bled with wounds to which time, the boasted healer, could bear no balm. This has taught those who have mourned over outraged love or wounding ingratitude, who have drunk deep of the Psalmist's cup of sorrows, and seen the nearest and the dearest—not the open enemy, but the familiar friend—turn against them or forsake them, yet to live on, in peacefulness and hope, patiently though longingly awaiting the time when the Great Shepherd shall call the weary and the way-worn into his everlasting fold. 'For our light affliction, which is but for a moment, worketh for us a far more exceeding and eternal weight of glory, while we look not at the things that are seen, but at the things that are not seen; for the things which are seen are temporal, but the things which are not seen are eternal.'[1]

But not only in the merely general characteristics of reversed attitudes and changed aspects, can we trace in the New Testament the altered idea of suffering, but in the more special detail of totally *fresh relations*,—relations which, when properly and seriously considered, will be found to include every highest form and phase of consolation. Time would

---

[1] 2 Cor. iv. 17.

fail me to enumerate all, but to three of these purely evangelical characteristics of suffering I earnestly desire to call your attention.

First. We have authority for saying that a condition of suffering, more especially in its purer and holier forms, calls forth the sympathy of Christ.[1] On this profound spiritual truth I will not now enlarge, further than to say, that when its full significance is fairly grasped by the mind, we have at once before us one of the most consolatory aspects which our finite powers can conceive it possible for suffering to assume. When we can truly feel that it is even so, that when we suffer we become the objects of a sympathy so vivid and so divine,—a sympathy that unites the two highest conditions under which such a sympathy can be conceived, perfect knowledge of all the miseries which sin has produced, and that perfect holiness which sympathizes without the admixture of a single selfish element,—when we truly realize this, we need no longer marvel that an Apostle could find ground of rejoicing in suffering, yea, and of boasting in tribulation and affliction. Thus considered, suffering becomes one of the most blessed boons which God can bestow in this world on those that love him. One of the deepest curses of the law has become one of the highest blessings of the Gospel.

Secondly, and further; we may dare to say that

---

[1] Heb. iv. 15.

not only does suffering in every purer form tend to call forth our Redeemer's divine sympathy, but that even beyond all this it binds us to Him in a strict and holy fellowship, that it draws the bonds of union yet closer between redeemed and suffering man, and his redeeming and once suffering Lord. Such assertions sound strange and bold; but have we not the strictest warranty from the New Testament for declaring that they are most vividly real, most unreservedly true? What else can the Apostle St. Paul mean when he writes from his prison at Rome to his converts at Philippi, and tells them that he counts all things but dung, that he may know Christ and the fellowship of His sufferings,[1] and realize in his own soul and spirit that holy and mysterious bond? What else can St. Peter refer to, when, in writing to the Christians of Asia he bids them rejoice in their fiery trial,—inasmuch as thereby they are partakers of the sufferings of Christ.[2] Sympathy is a near bond, but fellowship in suffering, drinking with the Lord out of the same bitter cup, and being baptized with His baptism, bearing in body or in soul the semblance of His cross, and entering the penumbra of a sorrow to which the world has seen no like sorrow,[3] is a nearer and closer union still,—a union that elevates all pure and holy suffering into all but the loftiest aspect in which it can be contemplated by man.

---

[1] Ch. iii. 10.   [2] 1 Pet. iv. 13.   [3] Lam. i. 12.

All but the loftiest aspect; for, *thirdly* and lastly, there is apparently one still higher aspect disclosed to us in the New Testament, under which we seem to recognise relations yet more mysterious, and issues yet more deeply consolatory. Not only is suffering presented to our contemplations as evoking the sympathy of Christ,—not only does it bind us to Him in a close and holy fellowship, but strange and almost awful to say, there is a text that seems to imply that holy human suffering can so far co-operate with the sufferings of our Redeemer, as to be daily and hourly working towards the consummation of all things, and to the hastening of the hour when the kingdoms of the world shall become the kingdoms of Christ. I allude to that profound passage in the first chapter of the Epistle to the Colossians, in which, when speaking of his sufferings for the Church, the Apostle uses these weighty words, 'I fill up the lacking measures of the afflictions of Christ.'[1] The exact meaning of these words has, I am aware, been the subject of much controversy: after mature deliberation, however, I can scarcely doubt that the passage was rightly explained by some of the early Reformers,[2] when they understood the afflictions of Christ, to imply not the personal sufferings of Jesus, which it were blasphemy to say could admit of any addition or supplement,

---

[1] Ver. 24, ἀνταναπληρῶ τὰ ὑστερήματα τῶν θλίψεων τοῦ Χριστοῦ.
[2] See note G.

but — the afflictions of Christ Mystical, of the Redeemer in His still suffering Church. The doctrinal inference, then, must be this; that holy human suffering, even in its individual manifestations, is all tending to one mighty end, all adding drop after drop into the fore-ordained cup of the sufferings of Christ in His Church; and that when the cup is fully filled up, when the last suffering has been endured, and the last sorrow over-past, the end will be nigh at hand, and He that cometh will come and will not tarry. Strikingly accordant with this, is a mysterious passage in the book of the Revelation, in which the souls of them that were slain for the word of God and the testimony which they held, are represented as crying out unto the Lord, to delay His vengeance no longer, and to hasten His judgment. And that exceeding bitter cry is stilled by the declaration that they were to tarry till the lacking measures of suffering should be filled up, and till the fore-ordained aggregate of the afflictions of the Church should be fully consummated: 'And it was said unto them, that they should rest yet for a little season, until their fellow servants also, and their brethren that should be killed as they were, should be fulfilled.'[1] If this application be correct, then is suffering finally presented to us in the most comprehensive and most consolatory aspects that it is possible for the mind of man to conceive;—most

---

[1] Rev. vi. 11.

comprehensive, because involving so close a connexion with the consummation of all things;—most consolatory, because assuring us that individual suffering, in all its higher and purer manifestations (more especially when seemingly undeserved, or transcending the ordinary limits of mortal misery), is neither unmarked nor inoperative, but that every pang and every tear have their issues in the hastening of the kingdom of Christ.

Oh! what real consolation this speaks to us when we turn our thoughts backwards, and muse on the tempest of unexampled suffering which broke over so many of our countrymen in the year just past.[1] When, in our blindness and dismay, we would almost arraign the justice of God for leaving the servants of His Son to have endured such extremes of pagan hatred, such cruelty, such malignity, how this thought stills us,— that all were filling up some of the yet lacking measures of the sufferings of Christ; yea, that not a pang of quivering flesh was fruitless, not one agony in vain. All added a few more drops to the cup of the afflictions of Christ, all ministered to the hastening of the hour when sorrow, and pain, and death shall be no more, and when they that have been partakers in their Lord's sufferings shall be called to His right hand to reign with Him for ever and ever.[2]

And here let us pause. Our meditations have now reached their climax, our speculations their furthest

---

[1] The year of the Indian Mutiny.   [2] See 2 Tim. ii. 12.

bound. We have seen that, which in its first aspects bore the brand of divine anger, become so changed in all its features as to appear at last a token of God's paternal love, a blessed assurance of the sympathy of Christ. That again, which once stood in close alliance with sin and death, is now seen to be one of the more mysterious bonds that unite all holy sufferers on earth with their once suffering and now glorified Lord. And, lastly, that which once seemed to be an alien element and disturbing force in the development of creation, is now a very part of the providential government of God, and a holy instrument in the furtherance of His kingdom.

In conclusion, permit me to offer a few sentences of homely exhortation.

To an audience like the present, composed for the most part of isolated members of distant and unconnected households, and consequently less directly acted upon by common sufferings or reciprocated sympathies, the application of our meditations must necessarily be somewhat general and inclusive. To you, my elder brethren, I will presume to urge the vital necessity of receiving and bearing the sufferings wherewith an all-wise and all-merciful God may be pleased to try our hearts, not only in a spirit of patience, but also in one of thankfulness and love. There are probably very few here present, especially among those who have lived half the allotted days of man's life, that have not been visited by suffering either in its holier form, as a part of the providential dispensation of God, or its more judicial aspect as the bitter, though now merciful chastisement of sin. Are they few among us, who, on the one hand, have had some experience in suffering in its more purely mental and spiritual characteristics? Have not our own sins, or the sins of others, cast shadows over our hearts, which no sun of future joys can, on this side the grave, ever wholly dispel? Have not old misdeeds often strangely found us out, suddenly confronted us in an hour when we thought not, and by the bitterness of unlooked-for affliction made us feel that verily there is a God that judgeth? Are they few again, on the other hand, who have experienced suffering under all those various circumstances under which it appears inseparable from the condition of fallen mortality? Have not most of us been sharers in its more touching manifestations? Have we not known what it is to lose those we have dearly loved, to have felt the pressure of dying hands, and to have gazed into dying eyes; and have we not felt in our after bereavement that dull anguish of heart, that strange combined feeling of mental and physical suffering, which none save those who have truly suffered can ever adequately conceive? Or, lastly, have we not known the mystery of physical suffering, the gnawing tooth of pain, the wrench of agony, the sleepless night, the weary day? Have we not every one of us had experience in some or all of these things? But let me ask, have we borne all with that holy resignation, that thankfulness and joy, which our present meditations seem so plainly to inculcate? Perchance not. I fear there is much in purely intellectual pursuits that often tempts men to exhibit more of Pagan endurance than Christian patience, to league with the outer world against the inward, or, worse still, to sit proudly down with their little handful of sorrows, soured and sullen, to wear the haughty livery of disappointment, and by the gall of bitter words and the peevishness of a repining tongue to show that God's calls have been worse than unheeded, that His fatherly love has been despised, and the holy and mystical sympathy of His Son either disregarded or rejected.

I greatly fear that, with mere intellectual men, it is often so,—perhaps to a far greater extent than we may at first be disposed to admit. But, at any rate, let it not be so with us. Here, at least, there are holier influences than those of mere intellect. Here there have been generations after generations of the patient and the brave, meek sufferers, true-hearted confessors, loyal martyrs,—men who despised not their Master's cross, nor thought lightly of His sympathy: and shall we individually in the hour of trial prove ourselves unworthy of such a spiritual ancestry? Shall we show ourselves callous and dead to the quickening memories of such examples? When the holy shadow of God's hand may next fall across our paths, may His grace be in our hearts; may we feel and acknowledge all purer suffering to be what it really is, a note of the sympathy of Christ, a token of His fellowship, a state of holy co-operation in hastening His kingdom, yea, an avenue to future blessedness and glory. For is it not written, and does it not remain, the enduring principle of the Covenant of Life, that they who walk in white must 'come out of great affliction,'[1] and 'that through much tribulation we must enter into the kingdom of God.'[2]

Again to you, my younger brethren, I would fain speak with all earnestness. Do not, I beseech you, cast aside the meditations of this afternoon as if they were something in which you had no interest,—as if the freshness of your health and strength, and the frank joyousness of a sunny heart, promised a long immunity from that which our text declares to be the certain heritage of mortality. Youth, brethren, is no guarantee against suffering: the very youngest among you may be summoned to enter into the cloud of pain, affliction, or trial, before the setting of to-morrow's sun. Mere courage, again, is but a poor staff to lean upon: for blameless in the eyes of God and men as is that frank bravery, which so commends you to one another, yet remember that to use it defiantly and proudly when God's hand is upon you, is to show yourselves rather children of Lucifer than the bravely-patient servants of Jesus; and is, in all respects, as grievous a sin as the vaunted philosophy or stoical indifference, which I have just specified as the peculiar temptation of older men. If

---

[1] Rev. vii. 14.   [2] Acts xiv. 22.

you are called in your young days to bear your Master's cross, steel not, I beseech you, your hearts against His divine sympathy; spurn not the unutterable blessing of a fellowship in His sufferings, and the august privilege of hastening His coming and His kingdom.

Above all things, put no false construction on my words. If the general tenor of the sermon has been consolatory, by its effort to demonstrate the different aspects of suffering under the Law, and under the Gospel,—yet remember that the iron link between sin and suffering remains unbroken. Remember, that, so surely as you sin, so surely shall you suffer. And oh! think of the melancholy bitterness in later life and maturer years, of clearly seeing by that frightful resemblance of the sin and the suffering, which is ever such a startling characteristic of all judicial affliction,[1] that it is your Cambridge sins that have at last found you out; and of feeling in your sorrow and shame that you carry remembrances which tears cannot wash away, and that you walk the earth bearing in your own bosoms a fearful witness to the certain chastisement, and cleaving curse of sin.

Such suffering, the suffering of the evil-doer and the sinful, an Apostle[2] has warned us has none of those holier aspects on which we have been meditating. By the grace of God, if borne with lowliness

---

[1] See note II.　　[2] 1 Pet. iv. 15.

and thankfulness, it may be overruled to blessed issues, and may ultimately minister to salvation; but it ever bears too close an alliance with sin and shame to be contemplated without the deepest melancholy and misgiving. It may engender sullenness, apathy, and utter deadness of soul, and then the last state will become even worse than the first.

If we are called to suffering, oh! let us pray, young and old, that it may be with Christ and for Christ; and then, however heavy the cross, however wounding the thorns, however lacerating the scourge,—all will seem light and endurable. It will indeed be the token of our Father's love; it will indeed be the mystic sign that we belong to the most blessed company the world has ever seen,—even those who have come out of great tribulation, and have washed their robes and made them white in the blood of the Lamb, and to whom the words of apocalyptic prophecy stand fast for evermore: 'They shall hunger no more, neither thirst any more; neither shall the sun light on them, nor any heat. For the Lamb which is in the midst of the throne shall feed them, and shall lead them unto living fountains of waters, and God shall wipe away all tears from their eyes.'[1]

[1] Rev. vii. 16, 17.

SERMON III.

THE DESTINY OF THE CREATURE.—DEATH.

Rom. v. 12.

By one man sin entered into the world, and death by sin; and so death passed upon all men, for that all have sinned.

THE forcible and comprehensive text which I have just read, will in some measure prepare you for the subject, to which, with the help of God, I purpose directing your meditations this afternoon. Our first musings on the law of Vanity, to which the creation has been subjected, naturally led us onward to some further reflections on the mystery of suffering; and these again seemed to suggest, and even to require of us, some consideration of a subject still more deep and mysterious,—the true nature, significance, and relations of Death. I am, indeed, well aware that I am entering upon the discussion of a subject that involves much that is perplexed and debateable, and that has ever been regarded as belonging to one of the more difficult portions of speculative theology: still, with the assisting grace of God, I will presume to pursue my onward course; more especially, as it is my earnest conviction that some of the recent investigations[1] of this subject have led to untoward issues, and that opinions relative to death are now daily gaining ground, which, it does not seem too much to say, are tending to undermine the very foundations of all vital Christianity. That comprehensive truth, which an earlier age wisely considered as the basis and substratum of all its teachings—viz., *that the universal dominion of death is the perpetual and enduring evidence of the corruption of our nature*—is now either secretly carped at or inferentially denied. As the true consciousness of sin has become more and more lost or impaired, so surely have the scriptural aspects of death, and their clear and vivid reflection of our lost and fallen state, faded imperceptibly away,—either, on the one hand, into mere materialistic recognitions of a common lot, or, on the other, into the wild and presumptuous anticipations of a false and morbid spiritualism. Let the higher degrees of conviction of sin be once lost in the heart, and the Christian teaching of the nature and significance of death will surely and speedily follow.

But, let us at once address ourselves to a systematic consideration of our present subject.

In the consideration of a theme so wide and comprehensive, it is difficult to know where to begin, and still more difficult, in the compass of a single sermon, to discuss, even superficially, the many ques-

---

[1] See note A.

tions that press themselves on our attention as we proceed onward in this extended domain of Christian speculation. We shall, however, probably follow the simplest if not the most logical course, if we first take a hasty survey of the problem which modern speculation has essayed to solve, and of the solutions which it has propounded. Then, with minds somewhat cleared and prepared, let us turn reverently to the general teaching thereon of Scripture, as derived from its most cardinal declarations; and thirdly, let us sum up all in a brief investigation and expansion of the important text which I have chosen as the general guide to our present meditations.

1. If we take our point of departure from the fundamental distinction between man and all other living creatures, to which I alluded last Sunday— viz., that man has a *personal* existence, while other creatures are but the conditioned individuals of their various *genera*,—it is impossible to stifle the feeling that the presence of death in our own race, especially in its more sudden and painful forms, is a strange and, at first sight, startling phenomenon. Nor do any general considerations, apart from Scripture, tend in any way to diminish the difficulty. Nay, they enhance it. For the more we dwell on the seeming prerogatives of our humanity, and the more closely we observe the distinct lines of demarcation between the dissolution of the component parts of a rational being, and the mere resolution of the life of the animal into the common life of nature, the more

persistently does this plain question present itself to our thoughts,—*Why, then, do we die?* Why are beings thus endued with the awful gift of personality subjected to the conditions and restrictions of the genera of a lower creation?

This, in fact, is the cardinal question in its simplest form; and to this question modern speculation will be found to have given substantially two answers,— the one, on the side of a somewhat coarse materialism; the other, on that of a proud and repulsive spiritualism. These it will be well for us briefly to consider, as both have more secret adherents than we may imagine, and as both really tend to set aside some of the more momentous declarations of Scripture, and to becloud the most consolatory aspects of our faith. If asked why we die, *the materialist* points to the analogy of all things around us, to the earthly elements of which our frame is composed, to the apparent law that dust must come to dust, and to the seeming impossibility of flesh and blood, even in a state of sinlessness, ever progressing to immortality. He bids us to take good note of all these common conditions, and to mark the pervasive action of all these general laws, and to rest assured that after all, death, properly considered, can be no curse, but is only a stage in a development, a crisis in a life-fever, a sleep that is to usher in more exalted powers of being, and a stronger and a fresher life.[1] Such an

---

[1] See n. 26 B.

answer, we may observe, has ever a *necessitarian* aspect. All ideas of providential interpositions become inferentially denied, all the blessed meaning of the Atonement becomes perverted or volatilized. It is of the earth, earthy; and to the earthy alone can it wear any semblance of plausibility or consolation.

The answer of *Spiritualism* is somewhat different, and perhaps, at first sight, somewhat more plausible. Death it tells us is neither a necessity nor a punishment. It is no fixed point through which the line of being must compulsorily pass, no necessary stage in a necessary progress,—but simply a providential interposition, a fore-ordained means of cleansing and defecation, a friendly entrance by which we are to pass from an outer world of darkness and corruption into an inner world of light and immortality. It regards the present union of soul and body as distinctly involving conditions seriously detrimental to true spiritual progress. But death we are told puts an end to this unnatural state; the bond is severed; the encumbering body is resolved into its connatural dust, while the spirit, unperturbed and disenthralled, realizes all its purest conceptions and all the highest tendencies of its being.[1]

Such is the answer; but, if considered for a moment, it will be seen at once to give rise to a question infinitely more difficult to answer,—' Why then was man so constituted, why were we born into a material

---

[1] See note C.

world at all?' And to this question, on the hypothesis of the encumbering and alien nature of the body, I cannot conceive any answer *can* be returned, that does not ultimately base itself on dualism, and will not, on discussion, be found to reflect some of the worst forms of Manichæan error.[1]

It might be thought that such views were wholly incompatible with revelation, and that their maintenance involved a real denial of all that was distinctive of Christianity. But alas! brethren, modern speculation has learned the wisdom of wearing the mask of revealed religion, and of stealing into the heart with the pass-words of inspiration. If we use against it the arguments of Scripture, it knows how much more effective it is to dilute rather than to deny, and it has found by experience that glosses serve its end better than unqualified contradictions. If we simply and honestly appeal to such passages as our text, in which the Holy Ghost has been pleased to declare the existence of the indissoluble bond between sin and death, both materialist and spiritualist join in telling us that we must reconsider our definitions, and search and see whether such passages as our text contain any reference to physical death at all; whether it be not rather to *spiritual* death, and to a state, and to conditions with which the body has nothing to do. Nay, more, if we urge passages in which the context shows that a reference

---

[1] See note D.

to physical death is indisputable, we then are told that the effect of the fall was only to give death a fresh aspect, and that what before was and would have been natural, has now received an ethical significance,[1] and thus far—but thus far only—has assumed the character of a punitive dispensation, and wears some of the reflected hues of a definite judgment, and of a primal curse.

Such is modern speculation. Such, alas! are views that find acceptance in many a heart that may never have formally investigated them. Such views are usually masked and disguised: they are often made to wear the outward trappings of Scriptural diction, they are often clad in other liveries, and are not at first sight always easy to be recognised; still of their mischievous existence in our popular literature and popular Christianity no patient and competent observer can entertain any reasonable doubt. Year by year our so-called forward thinkers are encouraging us to push sin and its intimate connexion with physical death more and more into the background of over-lived prejudices and outworn creeds:—'What has sin to do with death? Death is but a necessity of the flesh, or a victory of the spirit: why are we to fear death?' And with feelings and sentiments like these, thousands and tens of thousands in this country who bear the name of Christians doze out an apathetic life, librating unconsciously between dualism

---

[1] See note E.

and materialism, and never seeing death in its true aspects till it meets them face to face and discloses all, and then it may be all too late. The true nature of sin may have remained too long unrecognised; the need of a Saviour too long unfelt; and now that death is actually come, there may remain nought save a hopeless obduracy, or a passionate and perhaps unavailing amazement.

II. But let us leave these melancholy aspects of modern speculation, and turn to the plain declarations of the word of God. Yet let us carry with us two useful hints, which the foregoing speculations have indirectly tended to suggest. *First*, that Scriptural statements on the connexion of sin and physical death are commonly evaded by the assumption that spiritual death is alone alluded to; and, consequently, that we must be unusually careful not to press isolated passages, such as our text, as bearing upon *physical* death, until it has been made clear, either from the context or from the analogy of Scripture, that that form of death actually forms the subject of the passage. *Secondly*, let us not fail to observe that all considerations derived from Scripture lead us ultimately back to the time and circumstances, under which death first appeared in connexion with our race; and that until these are carefully examined and properly estimated, no deductions from isolated texts can be fully relied upon, or made use of with complete confidence in practical applications.

Let us then, in accordance with these hints, pause

somewhat before we make use of our text as a final answer to the question which forms the subject of our present meditations. Let us prepare ourselves for properly appreciating the full force of its declarations by first considering briefly some of the details of the Creation and Fall of man, to which it reverts,—and more especially the important preliminary question, whether death was from the first a condition involved in the very formation of man, and a necessity to which he was *designed* to succumb, or only a possible and avoidable contingency? The decision on this question is of great moment. For if the former alternative be true, the reference of our text cannot be simply and distinctly to physical death; if the latter be true, its testimony to the connexion of sin and that form of death is explicit and irrefragable. But let us not anticipate.

To begin then; I may first advert to what I have before had occasion to notice,—the strikingly different modes of production in the case of man and the lower animals. The words of Scripture seem scarcely to leave any reason for doubting that the lower orders of creation owed their origin to the infused vivific energies of the very realms they were hereafter to occupy. At the word of God, the waters teem with living creatures; the winged fowl fly in the expanse of heaven; the earth brings forth the living creatures that were ordained to occupy its surface. Earth, water, and, perhaps, air, are the mediate instruments of creation in the case of the animal world.[1] But how strangely and significantly different is the creation of man! Man is not called forth living and breathing from the womb of a mother-earth, like the creatures over which he was to have dominion. Earth only supplies the material; the life-giving element comes immediately and directly from God: 'And the Lord God formed man of the dust of the ground, and breathed into his nostrils the breath of life; and man became a living soul.'[2] Add to this the further declaration that, as regards the mystery of form, man bore the image and likeness of his Maker,[3]—and we have before us a revelation, in respect of the composite nature of man, of a distinctness that it is impossible to misunderstand, and of an importance that cannot be over-estimated. Fearfully and wonderfully was man made: on the one side the material body, on the other the vivifying spirit; out of their union emerges the human soul; all united by the most mysterious affinities, all enshrined in a form that is expressly declared to have been an image and similitude of the ineffable perfections of the triune God.

Is not the gulf between such a being and the rest of the animal creation indescribably vast? Are we indeed to believe with modern speculation that such a being would have died if he had continued in the perfection in which he was created? Does it seem natural, does it seem conceivable, that a fabric so

---

[1] See note F.   [2] Gen. ii. 7.   [3] Gen. i. 26; see note G.

rare and so marvellous was to be dissolved like that of the beasts that perish? Was such a fair monument of the creative wisdom and power of God designed originally to fall before the lower potencies of physical death? Is it not, and must it not be true, that even as the ancient author of the Book of Wisdom has declared, 'God created man to be immortal, and made him an image of His own eternity?'[1]

Conceding, as we may do, with Bishop Bull, that such an immortality was pendulous and imperfect,[2] and would have needed the application from time to time of renovating or conserving energies; can we still do otherwise, than with that great divine accept the opinion of Nicene and ante-Nicene writers, and unhesitatingly avow our belief,—that Adam, in his state of innocence, would not have died, but would have gone on from glory to glory, until at last, to use the noticeable language of Theophilus of Antioch, 'he would have become canonized or consecrated, and ascended from Paradise to heaven?'[3] How this progressive immortality would have been maintained, it is profitless to speculate: this much only it does not seem improper to say, that in our ordinary reflections on the subject, we far too much exclude from our remembrance the existence of the tree of life. Who shall say that this might not have been a natural means of immortality, the living minister of a living influence by which the *possibility* of dying—a

---

[1] Wisdom ii. 25.   [2] See note II.   [3] See note I.

possibility confessedly implied in the earthly nature of the body—might have become continually abrogated and cancelled,¹ until at last, all that was mortal might have been swallowed up of immortality? At any rate, it is very noticeable that after the sentence of death was passed on man, exclusion from the mysterious efficacies of the tree of life seemed necessary to ensure the fulfilment of the sentence. The words of the sacred narrative appear to imply that man had not yet eaten of the tree of life, and that even then, fallen as he was, it might not be too late to avail himself of its quickening energies; it might yet give a natural immortality to what was even more than spiritually dead. 'And the Lord God said, Behold the man is become as one of us, to know good and evil: and now, lest he put forth his hand, and take *also* of the tree of life, and eat, *and live for ever* . . . So He drove out the man, and He placed at the east of the garden of Eden Cherubims, and a flaming sword which turned every way, to keep the way of the tree of life.'²

But further, when we contrast the first threat in relation to disobedience with the words of the formal execution of the sentence, the foregoing remarks become still more confirmed and justified. When we dwell only upon the threatening declaration, 'in the day that thou eatest thereof thou shalt surely die,'³ it might seem fairly doubtful whether the death there

---

¹ See note J.   ² Gen. iii. 22, 24.   ³ Gen. ii. 17.

specified is to be regarded as *spiritual* or as *physical*. If, on the one hand, the simplicity of the narrative might be thought an argument for a simple reference to *physical* death; the indisputable fact, on the other hand—that, even according to the half-truth of the serpent,[1] man *did not* thus die on the day of his sin —seems to plead with equal force for an exclusive reference to *spiritual* death. When, however, with this threat, we combine the expressly physical terms of the actual sentence, ' dust thou art, and unto dust shalt thou return;'[2] and observe further, the subsequent exclusion from the natural means of immortality presented by the tree of life, the physical reference seems again so far to preponderate, that we appear at last to obtain this compound result. *First,* that the curse which followed on disobedience was *physical* death, the date of which was deferred; *secondly,* that this death had so far a *spiritual* or metaphorical significance, that it comprehended in it all the miseries, sufferings and privations, which increase the tendency to physical death; and that these, in strict accordance with the declaration of God, commenced the very first hour after the promulgation of the sentence.[3]

The only counter-argument of any weight lies in the argumentative form of the condemnatory words; ' In the sweat of thy face shalt thou eat bread, till thou return unto the ground : *for out of it wast thou*

---

[1] Gen. iii. 4.   [2] Gen. iii. 19.   [3] See note K.

taken.' Man, it is argued, must surely here be rather reminded of a natural destiny which he had aggravated, than apprized of an alien doom which he had newly brought upon himself and his race. The logical connexion, we are told, implies that a return to the earth must always have been the fore-ordained lot of one who had been taken from it: 'thou shalt return to the earth, because from it was thy original formation.' But to this it may be briefly answered, that the best ancient and modern Hebrew grammarians by no means admit this argumentative force to be here natural or correct. It is distinctly asserted by one whose name will ever remain honourably connected with Hebrew literature,[1] and who certainly had no theological interest in maintaining such an opinion, that the true meaning of the clause is not, 'for out of it wast thou taken,' but 'out *of which* thou wast taken;' the disputed word really being no conjunction, but an antiquated form of the relative pronoun. The verse thus considered has a powerful and tragic force. It reminds man of those elements from which he was taken, only to set before him how utterly he had failed in fulfilling his true destiny, how he had neglected the higher for the lower side of his nature, and how, instead of making what was perishable immortal, he had yielded himself up to the general powers of nature, and cast in his lot with the beasts over which he was created to have lordship and

---

[1] See note L.

dominion. 'In the sweat of thy face shalt thou eat bread, till thou return unto the ground out of which thou wast taken: verily dust thou art, and unto dust shalt thou return.'

Thus far, then, all general considerations derived from the history of the fall would seem to lead us to the conclusion that Adam, if he had continued in his state of innocence, would *not* have died, but that, owing to his disobedience, he *did* die, and subjected both himself and his race to a dispensation, which was for him at first only a possibility, but which his sin turned into a fearful and inevitable certainty. 'The wages of sin was death'[1]—death, in the most comprehensive sense in which the word can be understood,—vanity, misery, sufferings, dissolution in this world, and, if the promise had not gone before the sentence, death in the world to come.

These general considerations derived from the history of the first Adam are much enhanced if we reverently and devoutly raise our eyes to the second Adam, and meditate on a few of the deeper hints supplied by the Evangelical history.

In the first place, in what aspects are we to regard the death of our Redeemer? Are we to regard it with some unguarded thinkers,[2] as only an anticipation of what must have happened in the ordinary course of nature? Surely there is something abhorrent in the thought, something from which the

---

[1] See Rom. vi. 23.   [2] See note M.

heart recoils, ere the head has reflected on it. What! was the Holy One to see corruption?[1] Is it conceivable that He who had the power 'to lay down His life and power to take it again,'[2] could have lost by alien agency that which was His own as God,— yea, more, His own, His own eternally, as pure and sinless man? Well, indeed, does the author of the Epistle to the Hebrews remind us, that the Lord partook of flesh and blood, even as the children whom He came to save.[3] But *how* did He partake of it? Did not the second Adam take it of the virginal body of Mary by the quickening power of the Holy Ghost, even as the first Adam was formed out of the earth, and called into life by the breath of God? If it be true that the Lord received a substance from His mother, which the nature of that mother, as transmitted from Adam, had made capable of dissolution, is it not also irrefragably true, that it was a substance in which that capability had become cancelled and inoperative;—cancelled, because in Him 'there was no sin, neither was guile found in His mouth,'[4] inoperative, because in Him, as the God-man, there was an eternal tree of life from which nought, save His own boundless mercies, could even temporarily separate the nature which He had been pleased to assume. These mysterious analogies between him that first sinned and Him

---

[1] Psalm xvi. 10, Acts ii. 27.   [2] John x. 18.
[3] Heb. ii. 14.   [4] 1 Pet. ii. 22.

that alone was sinless, between him that disobeyed and Him that came to do His Father's will, are not without great meaning and significance.

We may further illustrate this solemn portion of our subject by briefly noticing the mystery of the Transfiguration. Setting aside all considerations of the immediate objects it was intended to serve,[1] and regarding it merely as a recorded fact,—a fact, be it observed, on which the synoptical Evangelists are peculiarly explicit, and to which, years after it happened, one of the eye-witnesses very distinctly alludes;[2]—viewing it thus simply and plainly, does it not seem to hint at the glory that was compatible with sinless humanity, does it not suggest deep thoughts of what, in different measure and degree, might have been realized in the sinless children of a sinless forefather? Though on such profound subjects it is ever well to speak with a holy awe and a guarded and reverential reserve, though it is not for darkened and sinful beings like us to draw daring lines of speculative demarcation between the prerogatives of a pure and spotless humanity, and the eternal potencies of an indwelling Godhead,—it still does not seem presumptuous to imagine that this wondrous event may supply a hint, a trace, a vestige, of what might have found an analogy in the uncorrupted nature of man.

We might perhaps append to this some hints

---

[1] See note N. [2] 2 Pet. i. 17.

derived from what the Evangelists tell us of the Lord's resurrection-body;[1] its seemingly material condition on the one hand,—seemingly material in some respects as that of Lazarus,—and yet its preternatural and glorified powers on the other; the mysterious continuance on earth for the extended space of forty days, and the final ascent of that holy body into the heaven of heavens. Such reflections, however, would require a far more extended and guarded investigation than can now be ventured on. Enough, perhaps, has already been said—I will not say to prove, but to illustrate the intimate connexion which all general considerations derived from Holy Scripture lead us to recognise between sin and all forms of physical death.

III. We are now in a position briefly to sum up all in an expansion of our present text, to which all the foregoing observations have been designed to contribute.

And now with what force and clearness does it speak to our hearts: ' By one man sin entered into the world, and by sin, death.' What death? Some mere synonym for a generally corrupt state? Some term robbed of all its significance? Never! Every speculation on which we have ventured renders such a conception inadmissible and impossible. All considerations derived from the history of the first, yea, and of the second Adam, are opposed to such perilous

---

[1] See ref. O.

dilutions. No! it cannot be. The text emphatically reveals to us this one certain truth, that, by the disobedience of the forefather, corruption, dissolution, and death came upon him and his children. The body, the material part, was to be resolved into its dust; the soul and spirit were to pass into the underworld. The harmonious bond was broken, the primal unity was dissolved. Man was lowered to the condition of the animals over which he was to have lordship, and, save in the return of the immaterial part to the God that gave it—'the spirit of man that goeth upward'[1]—he differed in nothing from the perishing beast, 'whose spirit goeth downward to the earth,' and whose life was being continually taken up and re-absorbed into the general life of nature.

Such was the disturbance of sin; such that dread dispensation which modern speculation would mask and disguise, and of which so many speak with such lightness and profanity. 'By one man sin entered into the world, and death by sin.'

But was this all? Had sin and has sin no further energies and activities? Did it only introduce a condition common to the race, that remains only a dismal and isolated fact on which in dull hours we may muse and speculate? Ah, no! Then were not sin, sin: then might death have had no real intensity, no true sting, the grave no completed victory. Hear further the distinct revelation of the text: 'And so

---

[1] Eccles. iii. 21.

death passed upon all men.' So,—in consequence of this relation between Adam's sin as the cause, and physical death as the effect,—death passed upon all men ;' or, if we would fain feel and understand the pregnant force of every word, '*passed through unto all men*,'[1] found its way to individuals, came unto every member of the race, often with untimely speed and aggravated violence, sought each one out, dealt with him singly, and made him in his very own body,—in his own perishing frame and in his own unhoused spirit, both feel and acknowledge the frightful power and pervasive energy of that principle which sin had called into action against our fallen and disobedient race. And lest man should proudly question the justice of such an universal sentence, or deny the equity of such individual application, this pervasive power of death is further confirmed by an appeal to the universality of that from which it sprung : ' Death *passed through* unto all men.' And why ? ' For that all have sinned ;' or, as we should perhaps more accurately translate the words, ' For that all *were sinners*,'[2]—sinners in the loins of their father Adam,—sinners as naturally descended from his body, flesh of the same flesh, bone of the same bone,—yea, more (for I doubt not that this also is included), sinners in their own persons, bearing witness by their very deeds, proving, by the sad testi-

---

[1] ἐφ᾽ ᾧ διῆλθεν εἰς πάντας ; see Meyer *in loc.*
[2] See *Revised Transl. of Rom. by Five Clergymen*, p. xii.

mony of similar acts of disobedience, that they are one in heart and one in passions with him who brought on himself and his race the penal judgment of death.

And ever since that first hour of lapse, this power of sin and death has been spreading and widening, developing itself in new forms, revealing itself in fresh aggravations: Adam handed down the fearful heirloom, not only to Cain the wicked, but to Seth the holy; and Seth to Enos; and Enos to those that followed him. And now, for nigh six thousand weary years, death has wrought and spread, augmenting itself by the sins of nations, races, kindreds, individuals; pervading all lands, corrupting all climes,—now by more frightful and generic manifestations, the flood, the fire, the famine, the sword, the pestilence,—now by the more gradual, yet ceaseless absorption of individual life (sixty lives or more, they tell us, each minute that goes past), making every child of man both feel and realize the sad heritage of mortality and the bitter bondage of corruption.

Such then, with all brevity, is the substance and meaning of the solemn text we have chosen for our meditations, such the answer we can now return to the homely though pressing question which suggested these investigations. . . . . If now asked *why we die*, we can answer it shortly and truly: 'We die,—not, on the one hand, because our nature was originally subject to that law, nor, on the other, because it is an appointed mode of emancipation from mere encumbering elements,—but, *because we are sinners*,—sinners in the loins of our father Adam, sinners in our own persons, witnesses in our daily thoughts and daily deeds of the exceeding justness of the primal sentence, and of the true righteousness of that dispensation which has subjected disobedience and rebellion to a judicial and punitive bondage.

And now I must draw my words to a close. There is, I regret to feel, much left unsaid; there are many illustrative topics, many mysterious analogies, which I have forborne even to hint at. That, however, which seems of chief moment I have done my uttermost to make clear; and I pray God that these two connected truths, which the present subject has mainly tended to disclose, may have found reception in your hearts: *first*, that if Adam had continued sinless he would not have succumbed to physical death; *secondly*, that when he did cease to be sinless he involved himself and his race in the common fate of the animal, which, to one constituted as he was, had all the attributes of a heavy and enduring curse. Upon the first of these truths, as Bishop Bull[1] has well observed, depends the proper recognition of the nature of the Fall; on the second, the conviction of the exceeding sinfulness of Sin, and of the depth of our own corruption.

Let me conclude with a few words of plain and practical application. The hortatory lesson which

---

[1] *Theol. Works*, vol. ii. p. 60, Oxford, 1827.

the tenor of our present meditations seems obviously to suggest, is to beware of being deluded into speaking or thinking lightly of a dispensation which our recent reflections have shown to be so truly fearful and tremendous. Of the large catalogue of spiritual sins there is scarcely any one more completely corrupting and perilous than that of viewing, either with a real or assumed indifference, the end of our mortality. Corrupting is it, because in all cases a failing and ever diminishing conviction of a future retribution will be found most surely to follow: making a mock at death has ever been found in closest connexion with making a mock at that of which it is the scourge and the chastisement. Perilous and soul-destroying is it, because from unchristian notions of death, the lapse to unholy and anti-christian notions of the nature of the mediatorial sacrifice and the efficacies of the Atonement is as certain as it is inevitable. . . . . All the more dangerous speculations on death to which the last twenty or thirty years have more especially given birth,—all those dead and driven leaves which the restless winds of a spurious philosophy have recently scattered across our pathways, tell only too plainly of the now stark and naked winter-boughs from which they have been blown,—a low estimate of the Atonement on the one hand, and a vaunting exaggeration of the so-called dignity of human nature on the other.

But in this place I need scarcely speak of such things. I will not and I cannot believe, that especially among the elder portion of my hearers, any disregard or light estimate of the unclothed state is viewed either with sympathy or toleration I do not believe that there is one graver thinker among us who would not agree with me in saying that there is only one aspect in which death does not seem absolutely intolerable, and that is, *dying in Christ*,—dying in Him who trod the death-realm before us,—dying in Him who tasted death, that whether we live or die, whether we remain clothed or unclothed, we should never be separate from His sympathy and His love.

Our only danger perhaps in this case, as in that of suffering, arises from the engrossing nature of our mental pursuits, and the facilities, which even our graver studies supply, of immersing ourselves in an absorbing present which makes the future seem far off, shadowy, and impalpable.

To the younger portion, however, of those among us, there is beyond all doubt an additional danger arising from inexperience in the deep realities of life, and more especially from false estimates of courage, and of what is, and what is not true Christian fortitude. To you, then, my younger brethren, let me more particularly address my closing words. Earnestly and affectionately do I beseech you not to fall into the temptation so common to your youth and inexperience, of holding cheap the frightful issue and evidence of the power and venom of sin. It is, alas! a matter of common observation, that the young and the high-spirited are ever sadly prone to think lightly of death and mortality. It is almost unnatural to expect it to be otherwise. They have as yet taken no deep root, they are full of enterprise, they love change. To them death often seems only a leap in the dark, a voyage to new shores, in which the very expected novelty is a set-off against the pain or the danger of the transit. It has ever been so. Yet yield not, I beseech you, to such common, yet such truly dangerous forms of temptation. Remember that there are two or three characteristics of death, which the holiest and the bravest have ever thought marked with exceeding fearfulness. . . . . To touch only the surface of such things, remember that in the dissolution of the material and immaterial parts of our nature, in becoming as the New Testament significantly terms it 'unclothed,' there is that from which even an inspired Apostle seemed in some measure to recoil. Yea, though in the fullest assurance that there was a house not made with hands, eternal in the heavens, the brave and true-hearted St. Paul could yet bear mysterious testimony to the shrinking of our nature from a purely bodiless existence. 'Verily,' saith he, 'we that are in this tabernacle do groan being burdened,—in that we would not be unclothed, but clothed upon, that our mortality might be swallowed up of life.'[1] Remember further, that there is in dying that which to all graver thinkers

---

[1] 2 Cor. v. 4.

ever seems above measure dreary and appalling,—its characteristic of utter loneliness and isolation. Hand in hand we go through life, sustained and sustaining; friends may be with us and around us even to the last; tender ministries may smooth the pillows of our death-beds; warm tears may fall on foreheads growing colder and colder with the damps of death,—but when the last is verily come, we are, and we must be, *alone*. There is no mortal companion along the valley of the shadow of death.

But last of all, and more than all, O bethink you of the dreadful nature of death when it comes upon you with sins,—the impure, coarse, and often deadly sins of youth either unrepented of, or perhaps yet flagrant in your soul. Then, indeed, does death assume every aspect of horror and amazement. To pass into the unclothed state is awful;—to pass into it in loneliness and solitude is appalling;—but to pass into it, perchance suddenly, in the whelming waters or on the foughten field, with a soul and spirit bearing scarlet traces of mortal sin, to bid farewell to the modifying conditions of time and space, and to enter, where there may be only one ever-present *here*, one never-ending *now*, is the most truly dreadful of all the dread aspects which it is possible for death to assume. '*Vere tremendum est mortis sacramentum.*'

Oh, then, may God in His mercy give us all His grace, that whether our years be many or few, we may all be brought daily nearer and nearer to Him,

—that we may become more largely partakers of the death-destroying power of His Son, more completely penetrated in soul and spirit with the quickening influence of the Holy Ghost; that so when the end come, we may pass there where 'there is no more curse,'[1] and where death hath been 'swallowed up of life.'[2]

---

[1] Rev. xxii. 3.   [2] 2 Cor. v. 4.

SERMON IV.

THE DESTINY OF THE CREATURE.—RESTITUTION.

REVELATION xxi. 5.

And He that sat upon the throne said, Behold, I make all things new.

THE consolatory declaration which I have just read, forms a suitable introduction to the mysterious subject towards which all our foregoing meditations have been tending to lead us, and to which all that has preceded has been designed to converge. The law of Vanity, even in the very passage in which it was enunciated, had its background of hope. Sufferings in their holier and purer aspects were seen to be prevenient and preparatory. Death derived all its deepest meaning from the fact that beyond it lay life and restoration. In a word, all the grave themes on which we have ventured to speculate, have been like secret hands leading us upward to a Pisgah of thought, from which the wide realms of the future kingdom of Christ might be surveyed in all their glory and universality.

Let us then for a brief space this afternoon yield ourselves to these natural guidings of our former subjects, and endeavour with all humility and sobriety to raise our eyes towards that which Scripture discloses to our gaze as lying beyond Vanity, Sufferings, and Death, even that for which all creation is now longing and tarrying,—freedom, renewal, and Restitution.

I feel, indeed, and deeply do I feel it, that I am now presuming to enter upon thrice holy ground,—ground whereon it is difficult for mortal speculation to enter without casting around some darkening shadows and defilements. Still, I also feel, that it is perhaps a duty that we owe to ourselves, not to shrink from a humble and reverential attempt to grasp the true outlines of a teaching which includes so much that is consolatory; and that, too, more especially, as there is no province in speculative theology in which modern thought has assumed more mistaken and more presumptuous attitudes. Much do I fear that, day by day, opinions more or less allied to that seductive form of belief called Universalism, or, in plain English,—the belief that all will come right at last, however wrong now,—are quietly winning their way among the children of this world's wisdom, and that they already number far more secret adherents than at first sight we may be inclined to believe. It takes but little ingenuity to trace it in many of the most popular literary productions of our own times. Poetry often scarcely masks it;[1]

---

[1] See note A.

many works of fiction seem almost written to give it currency; and, what is worse, much of the so-called religious philosophy of our own times, from which better things might have been hoped, does not shrink from avowing something more than a hope, that a time is coming when good and evil will lose their ineffaceable characteristics, and when all will be swallowed up in an abyss of love and restoration.[1]

Yet let us waste no time in confuting such notions. Here, at least, in this favoured place, the true issues to which such opinions ultimately lead,—the false logic from which they spring,[2]—the intense and frightful selfishness that they reflect,—the unholy compromise between things eternally incompatible that they necessarily imply,—must all seem well-nigh self-evident. The very youngest thinker among us who loves his Lord and keeps his sayings, can, I hope, have no real difficulty in arriving at the certain conviction that such things involve fundamental error. To confute them, then, or to expose them, is, I trust, in this place, both uncalled-for and supererogatory. Yet it may do us all good, especially in these dangerous days, if we spend a short time on those portions and passages of Scripture, of which such opinions are the distorted refractions; and if we further endeavour, by sober and Scriptural induction, to gain a true knowledge of what God's word tells us of this Resti-

---

[1] See note B.   [2] See note C.

tution, what appear to be its nature and characteristics, and what, if any, the necessary limits of its application.

Before, however, we proceed to the investigation of specific texts, let us, in accordance with that method which in discussions of this nature seems ever most sound and trustworthy, first prepare ourselves by a brief consideration of the general teaching of Scripture as to the original condition and constitution of man; that so, by a just estimate of what it once was, and what it now is, we may more truly appreciate the nature and measures of its future restitution. Then, further, remembering well the intimate connexion that ever subsists between man and the material world, let us venture to obtain some faint glimpses of the restoration and restitution of all with which man stands in any degree of contact, and with the future of which his own future is so closely and indissolubly connected.

When we turn backward to the account of the original formation of man, the first fact of importance, in reference to our present subject, seems clearly to be this,—that man was created single and alone. Though appointed to be the father and progenitor of holy and happy beings who,—as the old writers of the Church loved to speculate,—were to fill up the number of the lapsed sons of God,[1] he still appears single and isolated. The earth brings

---

[1] See note D.

forth abundantly, the waters teem with life, but man, the lord and sovereign of all, is presented to our view as coming from the hands of his Maker the single representative of his race,—even without the helpmate that was afterwards provided for him—*out of his own body*. This deserves our especial notice, this prepares us for the revelation of future unities more mysterious and comprehensive. Not only does the significant fact of man being a personal being, in contradistinction to the collective races of lower animals, at once emerge to view, but the still more profound thought of the *oneness* of the race; their oneness in creation,[1] their oneness in the sin of one, their oneness in the redemption by the One,— shall it not be, their oneness in restoration?

Nor does sin annihilate this unity of man's race. Nay, rather, as the sad experiences of our own hearts tell us, in some respects even more convincingly affirm it. Man transgresses against the positive command of his Maker,—that single command, so simple, yet so comprehensive,[2]—that command, to obey which was life and glorification; to disobey, death and corruption. Man transgresses, and all mankind transgresses with him: in Adam all die, even as in Christ all shall be made alive. In sin, mankind is still one. Yet sin undoubtedly presents to our view a phenomenon of the utmost importance in considerations affecting the universality of the resti-

---

[1] See note E. [2] See note F.

tution. Though sin does not cause a definite breaking-up of the race, it still discloses the continual divergence of individuals. It hints at fallings away from the great destiny of mankind,—the glorification of its Maker; yea, it shows dread glimpses of gatherings together under the banners of God's enemies, and of associations, which can have no share in the blessedness of future restitution. This is brought strikingly before us by the language of the first prophecy: "And I will put enmity between thee and the woman, and between thy seed and her seed."[1] Here, then, the existence of *two* seeds comes into view. Yet let us not misunderstand the words; not two seeds in any sense that might seem to imply that mankind had lost its unity,—that it was to be no longer one family, but two families, the one of the evil, and the other of the just.[2] That can never be: that would tend to rob this consolatory prophecy of the deeper reference that was ever ascribed to it by all the sounder thinkers of the early Church. The seed of the woman must ever point to Him in whom mankind was to be re-created and bound up in a living unity that was to endure for evermore. It marks no mere isolated family, no chosen few, but the race in its Creator and Redeemer, in Him who called it into being, in Him who was born of woman to save it, in Him who died for it, and in Him who shall restore it to a more than primal blessedness

---

[1] Gen. iii. 15. [2] See note G.

and perfection. It is so, and it must be so. Yet the fearful designation, 'the seed of the serpent,' cannot be without meaning and significance.[1] There must be some other seed, some other—I will not say community, but aggregation of evil beings, which has a real and substantive existence, and which displays its baleful vitality by its ceaseless warfare against the woman's seed, and Him who is Himself that seed and the Saviour of it: 'It shall bruise thy head, and thou shalt bruise His heel.' There *is* the serpent's seed; and in our future meditations let us not forget it: for earnestly and emphatically as we may dwell upon the unity of mankind and its summation in Christ, we still must not close our eyes to the fact that there are numberless, aye, appallingly numberless *individuals*, who are so deliberately sundering themselves from the living unity of their race and Him who is its head and representative, that *their* future, and the future of the true race, must be, and will be, eternally and irrevocably different.

This most important position, thus plainly deducible from the first page of the history of our race, admits of many illustrations from subsequent portions of it. How noticeable it is, when on the birth of her third son Eve uses language that seems to imply that Cain, considered as the representative of the race, was wittingly ignored; 'And she bare a

---

[1] See note H.

son, and called his name Seth, for God, said she, hath appointed me another seed—not *son*, but *seed*—instead of Abel, whom Cain slew.'[1] The unity of the race was continued in the 'appointed one:' the man that was gotten from the Lord[2] had severed himself from it, and was looked on as an alien and apostate. Then again, how significant is the fact, that after the flood the one man, Noah and his seed, form the continuation of the line of mankind. To the one man and his sons, God again vouchsafeth His blessing and His covenant. Generations pass away; the inhabitants of the earth multiply; but still it is to the *one* man, Abraham, to whom the promise is given, and to his seed after him. As the physical line was continued in Noah, so the spiritual line develops itself from Abraham; and with that one line, the God of all mankind is pleased to identify Himself as 'the God of Abraham, and the God of Isaac, and the God of Jacob.' Everywhere unity, nowhere division or plurality. One man, one seed, one stock, one nation, one centre and nucleus of developing humanity, even until the coming of Him in whom all again becomes one; and who, by His one sacrifice of Himself once offered, redeems all the race, and becomes henceforth and for evermore, not the Saviour only, but the representative of all mankind,—and who again, by His one Church, demonstrates that the same unity amid seeming plurality

---

[1] Gen. iv. 25.   [2] Gen. iv. 1.

is the mysterious law in the development of the kingdom of God.

Ere we completely leave the historical aspects of this portion of our subject, let me briefly subjoin, by way of corollary, a fact which I have before mentioned,[1] and which, in the wider applications of our present subject, it is desirable to retain steadily in view,—the intimate connexion between man and the animal and material world. In the very first day of his creation, man is indissolubly associated with Nature. Not only is he to have dominion over all that liveth, but he is to subdue and make his own the earth he treads on. When he falls, the earth becomes cursed; when the deluge sweeps off his race, the guiltless animals perish with him; when the covenant is made with the solitary surviving family, the surviving creatures are specially included in its provisions; the fowl and the cattle—every living creature of all flesh—share the blessings of the divine clemency. Even so it is impossible to doubt that when the restitution of man takes place, the restitution of the earth and its occupants will speedily and immediately follow. The day of the perdition of the wicked, as one Apostle tells us,[2] will let loose the last lustral fires, even as another Apostle[3] represents all creation waiting for its final redemption and glorification, as an event strictly and historically contemporaneous with the glorification of the elect of God.

[1] See Sermon I. p. 14.   [2] 2 Pet. iii. 7.   [3] Rom. vii

With these preparatory thoughts in our hearts, let us now turn to the special revelations vouchsafed to us by the Spirit in the New Testament, and with His illumining grace, let us endeavour patiently and reverently to deduce from them the nature and extent of the final restitution.

There are only three texts that seem to bear *directly* on this profound subject; but they are of a character so distinct that we may bless God for having afforded us thereby such sure ground for the highest aspirations and the most consolatory hopes that it is possible for the mind of man to conceive.

1. Let us begin with the lowest and most circumscribed of these texts, and proceed upward to that which is highest and most comprehensive.

The *first* passage is from that singularly profound chapter, the fifth of the Second Epistle to the Corinthians,[1] and the words to which I wish especially to direct your attention are these:—'*All things are of God, who reconciled us unto Himself by Christ, and gave to us the ministry of the reconciliation; for that God was in Christ,*—or according to the more plausible construction—*for that God in Christ was reconciling the world unto Himself, not imputing their trespasses unto them.*'[2] This most consolatory declaration forms the corner-stone of the doctrine of the restitution. It represents the nature of the first act, and the limits to which the benefit of the first act more par-

---

[1] Ver. 18, 19. [2] See note I.

ticularly extended. The first act was reconciliation,—reconciliation by the blood of Jesus; the first objects to whom it extended,—the world. Who shall dare to limit these words? Not even the great name of Augustine[1] shall deter us from saying that the blood of Jesus Christ—the blood that was poured out on Calvary—effected a reconciliation between God and *all* His intelligent creatures. No man was so far off, as then not to be brought nigh; no heart so estranged, as then not to be regarded with mercy and pity; no state so hopeless, as then not to come within the range of His all-merciful forgiveness. Then, indeed, did God enter into a new covenant with His own; then did He, who ever loved the creatures of His hand, love with all the depth of fatherly affection. His own Son, the Son of His love, died for mankind, and in that death all sin was forgiven. Yea, and the efficacy of that sacrifice remains undiminished and unimpaired: the restoration of the race has been commenced. Every year sees it evolving and expanding. Every generation, whatever cynical moralists may say, sees it advanced a step in its progress.[2] Amid all hindrance and obstruction, whether from within or from without, deadness of hearts or coldness of faith, worldliness and profanity, persecution and the sword, the Kingdom of Christ is still spreading; the elect are assembling; the hidden ones are gathering; the nations

---

[1] See note J.   [2] See note K.

of the saved are multiplying; the true spiritual unity of the race is coming more distinctly into view; reconciliation is making itself more sensibly felt in the deep heart of our common humanity. Salvation is verily come, and restitution will not tarry.

Four points of great moment this important text places before us: First; that a reconciliation has been and is effected between God and the world. Secondly: that the objects thus reconciled,—specified in the first portion of the passage by the more limited term *us*, and in the second by the more comprehensive term, *the world*,—must be regarded as neither more nor less than *all mankind*. Thirdly; that this reconciliation was effected by one mediating cause, and by one only, even our Redeemer Jesus Christ. Fourthly; and this, according to our present view of the construction, is what is noticeably characteristic of this passage,—that Christ was the personal sphere in which this reconciliation took place: that it was not only *by means of* Him, but *in* Him,— in Him and in His atoning sacrifice, in Him as the redeemer and true representative of humanity, that the divine agencies of reconciliation have their energy and existence.

2. With these results fresh in our minds, let us at once pass on to the second text, in which the subject of that which we have just considered is reaffirmed and reiterated, in language in some respects identical, but yet with expansions so remarkable and suggestive, that I will pray of you a close attention to the terms

in which it is expressed. This second text forms part of the first chapter of the Epistle to the Colossians,[1] and the words, accurately translated, are these; *'For in Him it pleased the whole fulness (of the Godhead) to dwell, and by Him to bring into former reconciliation all things unto Himself, having made peace through the blood of His cross,—by Him, I say, whether they be the things upon the earth or the things in the heavens.'*[2]

Now there are changes and additions in this mighty declaration that must have struck every attentive listener. The relation of time is somewhat changed; the nature of the reconciliation more exactly defined; its medium more emphatically specified; and the objects to whom this blessing is extended, more comprehensively enumerated. In our former text the reconciliation was mainly regarded as *past*; here the language seems to hint at applications more expressly *future*. The simple fact of the reconciliation was there dwelt upon; here, by means of a slight change in the flexible language of the original, the precise nature of that reconciliation, and the distinctly retrospective element it involves, are brought into unmistakeable prominence. There it was ' to reconcile;'[3] here it is ' to reconcile back again,'[4]— to bring back to a state of primal harmony,[5] and to re-establish a condition which existed when God looked with divine complacency on His creatures, when ' God saw every-

---

[1] Ver 19.   [2] See note L.   [3] καταλλάξαι.
[4] ἀποκαταλλάξαι.   [5] See note L.

thing that He had made, and behold! it was very good.'¹

Add to this, that in the former text it was an act of reconciliation which God wrought with reference to Himself,² and to the revelation of His own holiness and wisdom and glory: here, by a change which our language is scarcely sufficiently delicate to express, it is a reconciliation tending and leading *unto* Himself;³ not only a reconciliation but a reconciled access, — not merely a reconciliation regarded as ratified and solemnized, but one that brings the estranged ones to their Almighty Father's feet, and leads the lost sheep into the everlasting fold. Then again the holy medium by which it was brought about, which in the former text was noticed but not enlarged upon, is here brought into view, in language most exact and expressive. The reconciliation was to be wrought by Him,— by Him, the God-man, in whom all the fulness of the eternal Godhead was pleased to dwell. Yea more, and lest we might dream that it was some prior act contemporaneous with creation, or evolving itself from some former economies,— lest we should thus doubt, lest we should join with the sophists of our own days, and find only self-denial in what was salvation, our present text assures us that it was by the *blood* of Jesus, the blood of the cross, the blood poured out on Calvary, that the

---

¹ Gen. i. 31.   ² καταλλάξαι ἑαυτῷ.
³ ἀποκαταλλάξαι εἰς αὐτόν· see notes *in loc.*

mighty working was brought about whereby God bindeth in harmony all things unto Himself. And last of all, what in the first text was described as the world, here receives the noticeable amplification, 'whether they be the things on earth or the things in heaven,'—a definition so comprehensive, that I see not how we can dare to do less than regard it as embracing the sum of all things, the universal realm of creation.

What limitations, if any, the analogy of Scripture and the express terms of our allied texts compel us to assign to the actual realization and enjoyment of this reconciliation, let us for the present leave unnoticed. Let us, however, meanwhile not fear to say, that the efficacy of the blood of our Lord and Master is limitless in its applications, that it knows no bounds in space, as it knows no bounds in time; and that the issues of His atonement for us, in different measures and degrees, extend unto all things,—that the odour of that sweet-smelling savour fills every court and every chamber of the universal temple of God.

3. And now, before we make any general deductions, let us pass on to the third text,—the farthest reaching and most profound of all. The passage to which I desire, in the last place, to call your attention, forms part of the first chapter of the Epistle to the Ephesians;[1] and the words, carefully rendered, are these: '*Having made known unto us the mystery of*

---

[1] Ver. 9, 10, 11.

His will, according to the good pleasure which He purposed in Himself, in regard of the dispensation of the fulness of times, to sum up again (for Himself) all things in Christ, the things in the heavens, and the things upon the earth,—even in Him, in whom we were also chosen for His inheritance.[1] Now, on dwelling with attention on this most profound revelation, we cannot fail to observe that it leads to something beyond the furthest bound we have hitherto reached. The vast issues which are here disclosed to our view are distinctly prospective and future. Their first commencements, indeed, may have already taken place; the first motions of aggregation may have been already felt in the Church of God; the attracting energies of omnipotence may even now be working through all the realms of the spiritual and material world,—but, beyond doubt, the main aspects of the revelation before us are all distinctly *future*. Reconciliation was the first stage; reconciliation to a prior state of harmony, the second; summation of all things to and into Christ, in a word, restitution in its fullest sense, the third,—the final end and aim of the eternal counsels of God. And this restitution is to be boundless in its comprehensiveness. It is to extend, as the expressive words again remind us, to 'all things,—the things in the heavens, and the things upon the earth.' The uncircumscribed nature of the terms again forbids us to narrow what God has left broad, and

---

[1] See note M.

solemnly suggests, that as the efficacies of Christ's priesthood were without bound, so His kingly power (which this text seems more especially to contemplate) shall be as limitless, extending beyond the bounds of His mediatorial session at God's right hand, and enduring onward into that infinity when God shall be all in all.[1]

But further; if this reunion shall be thus collective,—if the objects of it shall be thus countless and universal, yet let us not fail to observe with what force and pertinence our present passage re-echoes the vital words, which were also characteristic of the first text, even the vital words, '*in Him.*' As our second text dwelt mainly on the '*by Him,*' or the mediation of His blood, so this last text dwells, with most noticeable emphasis, on the '*in Him*'—on incorporation in Him,—an emphasis which the repetition of the words 'even in Him,' seems especially designed to enhance. Yea, it would not seem presumptuous to say, that it is as if the design of the Holy Ghost were to make us feel distinctly, that to what lies *out* of Him and *apart* from him,—be it mortal or immortal, human or angelical, no efficacies of consummating love can be properly conceived to extend. Surely there is an implied limitation in the very statement of the universality that cannot be gainsaid; surely the possibility remains that there may be a *without Him.* Surely there may

[1] See note N.

be manifold states of confirmed sinfulness, frightful attitudes of enduring hostility against divine love, petrifactions of ingratitude, embodiments of sin against the Holy Ghost, to which the attractive energies that sum up all things in Christ may prove, owing to the dread mystery of the freedom of the will,—wholly inoperative. There is the *without;* and the individuals that belong to the outer darkness of that fearful realm, must remain the subjects, indeed, of the power of the Eternal Son, but from their appalling antagonisms, the monuments of His omnipotent justice.

Let us now, with all brevity, gather up into a few distinct allegations the results of our deductions from both Testaments,—both from the historical notices of the Old, and the express doctrinal declarations of the New Covenant. And they would seem to be as follow:—That a recognition of the true unity of our race is one of the fundamental requisites for properly understanding and realizing the doctrine of the restitution. That as all mankind are one in Adam, so are they, in a far higher degree, one in Christ; still, that as there were originally distinct traces of sinful severances from the true unity of the race, so is it now. That there is, indeed, a present general reconciliation, even as there shall be hereafter a universal restitution; but that as the reconciliation was not only *by* Christ, but *in* Christ, so, even more distinctly, is it said, that the restitution shall be *in* Him, and only *in* Him. Consequently, that all, which from the nature of things and the truceless opposition between light and darkness, between sin and holiness, cannot, without blasphemy, be conceived as *in* Him and in union with Him, will in the end be only as the dross and scum that is purged off by the refining and sublimating flame.

If it be urged against these allegations, that they really tend to do away with that very universality which they affect to assert, we fear not to answer, that it must be so; that we cannot, and dare not, close our eyes to limitations, which the very terms of these profound revelations distinctly presuppose, and which the whole analogy of Scripture forbids us to deny. If, on the one hand, restitution is in Christ, and in Him alone;—if, on the other hand, there be such a state as the second death, and one sin *at least* for which there is to be *no* remission, —then to assert that apostate angels in the abyss, and the seed of the serpent among men shall share in the blessings of the restitution, is practically to make a mock at the express declarations of the Word of God. In plain terms, is it not to avow a belief that what by its own ever increasing wilfulness and desperation has passed out of the sphere of attracting love, shall, by a violence that a wise father of the Church has declared is hateful to God,[1] be compelled to return to it,—that the cursed, whom the Lord shall have bidden to depart from Him into

---

[1] See note O.

the realms of His wrath,[1] shall be yet forced back to the arms of His love,—that the worm that dieth not shall die,—and that forgiveness shall be meted out to that for which it has been solemnly declared there shall be *no* forgiveness, neither in this world nor in the world to come. From such denials of what is written may God deliver us.

This much, however, we may dare to say, but no more than this,—that all, that from its union with the Saviour is saveable, shall be saved; all, that from being one with the Restorer is capable of restoration, shall be restored; yea, all that distinctly evinces the continued and preponderating action of the true central force, shall be gathered up into the ever blessed centre of Life and Love. To say more than this, is to do violence to revelations that carry with them their own limitations, and to expose ourselves hereafter to the appalling charge of having dealt deceitfully with the most express declarations of the unchanging Word of God. Doth it not stand written, brethren, and that too on one of the most solemn pages of the Word of God, that if 'it come to pass when a man heareth the words of this curse, that he bless himself in his heart, saying, I shall have peace, though I walk in the imagination of mine heart, to add drunkenness to thirst, the Lord will not spare him, but then the anger of the Lord and His jealousy shall smoke against that man, and all the curses

---

[1] Matth. xxv. 41; see note P.

that are written in this book shall lie upon him, and the Lord shall blot out his name from under heaven."¹

In the last place; *how*, and in what precise way, this restoring power of reconciling love shall work out its issues, has not been expressly revealed.

With regard to *ourselves*, a glance within at our state of inward discord and corruption affords us some elements for forming a conjectural judgment. . . . Shall not the will lose its contrariant force, and become one with the will of God? Shall not the spirit avow its heavenly origin and cleave unchangeably and indissolubly to the eternal Spirit of God? Shall not the affections of the soul become elevated and purified? Shall not the future body be such a soul's and spirit's fitting tenement; and excellent in strength, glorious in form, and expedite in celerity, approve itself to its Maker all, and more than all that it was before? And shall not the whole man, body, soul, and spirit completely realize that perfection of unity that shall render man creation's noblest image of the one God, the brightest mirror of His Maker's glories, and the loftiest exponent of His praise?

With regard to the effect of the restituent powers of Christ on the two extremes of creation,—the holy angels on the one hand, and the lower realms of nature on the other, so little has been revealed that it seems almost better to be silent than speak.

¹ Deut. xxix. 19, 20.

Perchance, however, those Sons of the morning, as St. Paul seems to hint in the third chapter of his Epistle to the Ephesians,[1] may be illumined with a yet higher knowledge, and be permitted to see into those deep mysteries of redeeming love which they desire to look into,[2] but may not yet fully know. Perchance the counsels sealed in silence from eternity may then be more completely revealed, that so with a yet fuller unison and a yet louder acclaim, they may for ever sing the power and wisdom of the everlasting King. 'And all the angels stood round about the throne, and about the elders and the four beasts, and fell before the throne on their faces, and worshipped God; saying Amen: Blessing, and glory, and wisdom, and thanksgiving, and honour, and power, and might, be unto our God for ever and ever.'[3]

Perchance, too, after the purging fires have burnt away from the material earth all the seeds of sin which the flood could not wash away, there may come forth out of its productive bosom races of living creatures, that in all their instincts, capabilities, and existences may ceaselessly glorify the creative wisdom. Perchance grass and flower and tree may again clothe the renovated earth, and in all their developments and through all their changes may so reflect the restoring power of their Maker, that they, too, may

---

[1] Eph. iii. 10; see notes *in loc*. [2] 1 Pet. i. 12.
[3] Revel. vii. 11, 12.

be permitted to bear their part in creation's new and universal hymn. . . . And then at length shall all that the creature sighed for be granted, all that it tarried for be fully come. 'And every creature which is in heaven, and on the earth, and under the earth, and such as are in the sea, and all that are in them, heard I saying, Blessing and honour and glory and power be unto Him that sitteth upon the throne and unto the Lamb for ever and ever.'[1]

Finally, permit me to offer a few sentences of earnest warning and exhortation.

If, brethren, the tenor of this sermon has been mainly re-assuring and consolatory,—if a mortal speaking to his fellow-mortals has shrunk from flinging broadcast denunciations of eternal Wrath while meditating on counsels of eternal Mercy,—if a sinner preaching to sinners like himself has shuddered at pronouncing avenues of mercy irrevocably closed, which a just deduction from the word of God leads us to believe are yet open,—if it be so, I nevertheless implore you not to misunderstand these words, and not to find in them the expression of hopes and expectations, which (God knoweth) they are not intended to convey. Remember, I pray you, that on being *in* Christ, on being yet within the sphere of His attracting and redeeming love, all depends. The question of all questions is, Are we in any sense *in Christ?* Are we united to Him? Is

[1] Rev. v. 13.

our will with all its changes and contrarieties still mainly one with His? Do we love Him? Is His that face which when heaven and earth shall melt away we long to gaze upon for ever and for ever? If it indeed be so, let us be of good cheer: He will never forsake His own; His reconciling power has had its effect on our hearts, His restoring powers will not eventually be withheld from us. If, however, the name of Christ is a name to us, and a name only; if deadly and unrepented sin has been tending to remove us further and further from Him; if there is that worldly stupor that usually merges into a complete insensibility to all the blessings of reconciling love,—then let us beware. There is a *without;* and to them who deliberately stand there, who have thus torn themselves from the stock of their humanity, who have wittingly withdrawn themselves from the sphere of their Master's love, and count His blood an unholy thing—there cannot be, if they die as they live, any share in reunion or restitution.

We may now positively shudder at the thought of ever being thus withdrawn from the attraction of divine love; we may now count it well-nigh impossible; we may yet feel a lingering gravitation within, which may seem to assure us that the effects of the central force are still perceptible, and we may trust it will be ever so. And we may trust to this last residuum of vital force to save us at the last. But will it be there then? As there are forces in the natural world which diminish with startling disproportion to the increasing distance, so it may be in the spiritual world. With sin, on the one hand, deepening, accumulating, intensifying, ever tending more and more into complete sinfulness, ever drawing us by slow and silent action into that increasing aversion to what is holy and good, which has always been regarded by all deeper thinkers as the dread harbinger of final impenitence,[1]—with such tendencies on the one hand, and, on the other, with a fast diminishing attraction toward the great Centre of life, who shall dare to trust that a future day shall find him in a sphere where reconciliation and restoration may still be possible and realizable? It is idle, it is hopeless. 'Behold, *now* is the accepted time; behold, *now* is the day of salvation.'[2]

May God, then, of His mercy grant that His grace may work in our hearts with renewing and renewed energies. May the love of our Master become to us a more vital and attracting force than we have hitherto felt it. Amidst all hindrances and amidst all temptations,—during all darker seasons of doubtfulness and despondency, in the watches of the weary night, when unwonted forms seem walking the waters of our souls, may we ever hear the reassuring voice of love and mercy, 'It is I, be not afraid.'[3] Borne up by that arm, who shall fear? reconciled by that love, who shall be dismayed? Though worlds shall dissolve and the heavens pass

---

[1] See note Q.   [2] 2 Cor. vi. 2.   [3] Matth. xiv. 27.

away, no soul that is truly drawn towards Him shall be finally separated from His mercy and love; no man or devil shall pluck us out of His hand : 'For I am persuaded that neither death, nor life, nor angels, nor principalities, nor powers, nor things present, nor things to come, nor height, nor depth, nor any other creature, shall be able to separate us from the love of God which is in Christ Jesus our Lord.'[1]

---

[1] Rom. viii. 38, 39.

SERMON V.

THE THREEFOLD NATURE OF MAN.

1 Thessalonians v. 23.

And the very God of peace sanctify you wholly; and I pray God your whole spirit and soul and body be preserved blameless unto the coming of our Lord Jesus Christ.

THE words, brethren, which I have just read, have a grave claim on our attention. From the days of Irenaeus[1] down to our own, this text has been confidently appealed to as an emphatic statement of the elements and constituents of the nature of man. Though amidst much diversity of interpretation, and much variety of exegetical detail, it has still ever been regarded by thoughtful men as a distinct and almost formal exposition of the mysterious economy of our being: it has been deemed a clear and authoritative statement of the triplicity in unity of human nature, and a witness that may not be gainsaid of the existence and association of three elements in man, body, soul, and spirit.

[1] See note A.

On texts such as these it is at times wise to meditate. It is well for us, especially in the graver hours of a penitential season like that in which we now have entered, to seek out the more retired sources of Scripture truth, to court the keener but more bracing airs of doctrinal investigations, and, in the reverential contemplation of the higher mysteries of our faith, to forget for a while the wearisome subjectivities of that undemonstrative theology, which is alike the characteristic and the bane of our age. I make no apology for introducing this peculiar subject to your notice; for though, at first sight, it may seem of a purely speculative nature, it will still be found, on a nearer survey, to be truly and essentially *practical*; it will often be found to throw a strangely and fearfully illustrative light on the more common forms of temptation which try our souls; it will often give us some blessed glimpses of the operations of the eternal Spirit of God within us; it will often add a deeper significance to the varying, and only too commonly unnoted phases of our inner life.

I cannot, indeed, hope to dwell upon these powerful applications, for I fear that the mere discussion of the text will occupy nearly all our time, but I shall still rejoice in the feeling that, in bringing such question before you, I am not asking you to meditate upon a mere sterile thesis, but on a subject whose seed is in itself,—a subject which cannot fail to make us more conscious of the infinite mysteries of our being, and more sensitively alive to the tidings of that sore strife, that fell and utter conflict of the Flesh and the Spirit,[1] of which the soul of every one of us in this church is the theatre and the battle-ground.

Nay more, such a subject as the present has a pressing claim upon us, not only from its own importance, but from its vital connexion with some of those doctrines which, in our own day, we have seen brought into prominence, and which, full surely, another generation will recognise as its questions of most serious import, the doctrine of the Last things, —eschatology, as it has been termed,—and the doctrine of the Atonement. With these our present subject has the most intimate connexion; and it would not be too much to say, that nine-tenths of the hasty assertions which we have seen put forth upon these doctrines would have been completely avoided, if a little more attention had been paid to the fundamental constitution of our common nature, and the true nature and interdependence of its three mysterious components, Body, Soul, and Spirit.

The ignorance of the scriptural aspects of this question, and the complete disregard which the whole subject of biblical psychology has experienced, is no less startling than demonstrable. In but few of our recent commentaries, or theological treatises, is there any attempt to distinguish between the characteristics of our psychic and spiritual natures. Scriptural terms of such usually distinct significance as ' heart, soul

---

[1] Gal. v. 17; see notes *in loc.*

mind, understanding, inner man,' meet with the most varying interpretations; nay, the only epithet which a common and popular assent has associated with one part of our common nature, 'immortal' soul, is either insufficient or of doubtful application;—insufficient, if the term soul be used as including our whole saveable nature;[1]—of doubtful application if it be used in its more precise and restricted significance.[2]

But it is time that we approached the text itself. The words which I have chosen for our consideration form part of one of the concluding verses in the last chapter of St. Paul's 1st Epistle to the Thessalonians,—a chapter of an unusually grave tone, and marked in its latter portion by an emphatic brevity, and a striking solemnity of exhortation. The context does not supply anything to guide us clearly in our interpretation; unless, perhaps, the momentous warning in the 19th verse, 'quench not the Spirit,' led the Apostle to pray fervently in the 23rd, that the temple in which that holy flame was burning might be preserved in its integrity and blamelessness until the coming of the Lord,—that the spirit, and soul, and body, of his converts, each in its full measure and completed proportions (ὁλόκλ ον), might await the searching scrutiny of the final judgment. This connexion of the admonition in the 19th verse with the prayer of the text, will perhaps afford a hint when we

---

[1] See note B.   [2] See note C.

come to consider specifically the meaning of the term *spirit*; but in the general survey the most important point is the recognition of the peculiar position and correct grammatical construction of the epithet *whole*,[1] and the preservation of its exact meaning.[2] For observe, the position of the epithet shows that the prayer is not (as the ordinary reader of the Authorized Version, or the uncritical reader of the original might be led to imagine) that the *whole* spirit, soul, and body, the three associated together, may be preserved, but,—that each part may be preserved *in its completeness*. Not mere associated preservation, but preservation in an individually complete state, is the burden of the Apostle's prayer. The prayer is, in fact, threefold; *first*, that they may be sanctified by God, the God of peace—for sanctification is the condition of outward and inward peace —wholly ὁλοτελεῖς, in their collective powers and constituents; *next*, that each constituent may be preserved to our Lord's coming; and *lastly*, that each, so preserved, may be entire and complete in itself, not mutilated or disintegrated by sin:— that the body may retain its yet uneffaced image of God, and its unimpaired aptitude to be a living sacrifice to its Maker; the appetitive soul, its purer hopes and nobler aspirations; the spirit, its everblessed associate, the Holy and eternal Spirit of God.

[1] See note D. [2] See note E.

This analysis of the passage will be found of considerable use, when we have to attempt to decide between the different interpretations which the text has received; and still more so, when we further attempt to substantiate the differences and elucidate the distinctions between the three elements of our nature, of which this important text makes such a certain and significant disclosure.

Resting on this analysis, let us proceed with our subject, which will here most naturally divide itself into two parts; First, an attempt to establish the assertion that Scripture generally, and this text in particular, contemplate the nature of man as compounded of three principles, spirit, soul, and body: Secondly, an attempt to trace out the scriptural distinctions between the functions of each component part.

And here, at the outset, let us observe, that we may somewhat simplify the subject by confining ourselves on the present occasion to the consideration of the two former principles, spirit and soul; for to doubt that the *body* is an integral part of our nature, both here and hereafter, is to indulge in either a wild Manichaeism, or a still wilder Docetism, which deserves neither attention nor confutation.

By thus confining ourselves simply to the consideration of the spirit and the soul, we gain this great advantage, that we may reduce our whole subject to two simple inquiries; *First*, Does this text and Scripture generally recognise such a difference between soul and spirit that each may be considered a separate, or, to speak more cautiously, a separable element of our nature? *Secondly*, if so, what meaning does Scripture assign to each term, and what does it reveal of the nature of each, and of the sphere of its operations?

I. With a text before us so plain, so emphatic, as that now under our consideration, it does seem hard indeed to be forced to pause in our answer to the first inquiry. We must not, however, ignore the fact that it has been asserted[1] that the text has simply a cumulative and rhetorical character, and that the Apostle in thus grouping spirit, soul, and body, meant only to imply, without any further distinction, the material and immaterial part of them for whom he prayed; that spirit and soul, in fact, is a rhetorical tautology.

But is this tenable? Is this possible? Is this in any way consistent with our analysis of the text? If the Apostle prays for the sanctification of his converts in their collective powers and parts (ὁλοτελῶς,—if he further prays with a studied emphasis and peculiar collocation of words, that three things may be individually preserved whole till the advent of the Lord, —and if, of these three things, the two latter, soul and body, are confessedly constituent parts of that nature for whose entire sanctification he prays,—does it not seem almost monstrous to doubt that the third, or I should rather say the first part, thus similarly

---

[1] See note F.

connected, thus similarly enunciated, thus significant in its very precedence, is a constituent part as well? Surely we do violence to the plainest principles of perspicuity if we assign any other meaning to the text than this,—that the Apostle prayed for the conservation of the spirit as well as the conservation of the soul of his hearers, and that in so praying he regarded them as in a certain degree distinct from one another.

But is this a mere isolated text, on which it may be unsafe to base a system of psychology? Can no other passages be fairly adduced in which the terms soul and spirit are placed in a juxtaposition that is neither cumulative nor rhetorical? Does Scripture elsewhere preserve a studied silence? By no means: though, as we might have easily imagined beforehand, the passages which involve a comparison of a material with an immaterial part are far more numerous than those in which the two immaterial parts are compared or contrasted, we nevertheless can still adduce several passages, which can be neither thoroughly nor satisfactorily explained, unless we recognise a real and appreciable difference between the soul and the spirit of man. Let us here, however, be careful to follow the rules of an honest criticism. Let us make no use of such passages as have either a poetical character, or involve such a studied parallelism, as make it doubtful how far a real difference of meaning was intended by the inspired writer.

Let us then not press such passages as that of

Isaiah,[1] 'With my soul have I desired thee, with my spirit will I seek thee early;' or again those familiar words of the Virgin's hymn, 'My soul doth magnify the Lord, and my spirit hath rejoiced in God my Saviour;'[2] though in this latter case it is certainly worthy of notice, that it is the soul which magnifies, the spirit which rejoices. It is the soul, the true mediatrix between the body and spirit, which by means of the bodily organs gives outward expression to the joyful conceptions of the spirit. . . . Yet let us concede that these and such as these, are texts of a strain too elevated and too poetical to be safely subjected to ordinary criticism. Let us pass them by, and rather seek out passages of a more decided doctrinal aspect, and see in them how far this difference between soul and spirit can be fairly maintained. Let us appeal to a profound verse in the fourth chapter of the Epistle to the Hebrews,[3] where the word of God is said to pierce so as to divide soul and spirit (not soul *from* spirit, according to the ordinary gloss,[4] joints and marrow. Now in this difficult verse, whatever interpretation we may assign to the latter terms, whether we regard the meaning of joints and marrow as simple or metaphorical, we seem equally forced to recognise a distinction and a difference between the former terms,—the spiritual regions through which the word of God pierces its way. We seem empha-

---

[1] Chap. xxvi. 9.   [2] Luke i. 47.
[3] Ver. 12.   [4] See note G.

tically told in language of startling power, how that word penetrates, beyond the sphere of the affections or impulses of the soul, into the realm of the wakeful and watchful contemplations of the spirit, and there in the light of clearest day carries on the controversy of God, and forces man to his final, and it may be irrevocable decision for or against the Gospel.[1]

We cannot utterly overlook such passages as that in the first chapter of the Epistle to the Philippians,[2] where the Apostle expresses his hope that his converts are standing in one spirit, certainly not the Holy Spirit, with one mind (soul it should be translated) striving together for the faith of the Gospel,[3]— especially when in such a passage we further observe with what significance an expression of passivity is used in connexion with the serene spirit, and of activity with regard to the more impulsive soul. And to take a final instance; when, in the fifteenth chapter of the first Epistle to the Corinthians, the Apostle declares that, 'it is sown a natural (literally psychic) body, and raised a spiritual body,'[4]—what else does he mean than that it is sown in a state in which the soul sustains the principal, and the spirit the subordinate part, but that it is raised in a state where those conditions are exactly reversed.[5]

What a light does this verse throw on the whole subject of our constitution both here and hereafter!

---

[1] See note II.   [2] Ver. 27.   [3] See notes *in loc.*
[4] Ver. 44.   [5] See note 1.

But to leave special quotations, may we not appeal to other arguments of a more indirect character, but of no less force and cogency? Is it not very noticeable that in the frequently recurring contrasts of our material and immaterial natures,—contrasts which at first sight might be thought only to imply a twofold nature,—the terms regularly opposed to each other are of such a kind as really to give to the assumption of a threefold nature a very high degree of plausibility. Observe, it is ever the flesh and the spirit, the soul and the body, which stand in respective opposition to each other; and with the exception of a very few passages, in which, indeed, a most satisfactory reason can be assigned for the change, this law of antithesis is never violated.[1] Let us pause a moment to notice how instructive these oppositions are, especially when we remember the vast scriptural significance of the term *flesh*; how it comprehends, not only the mere sensual desires, but all motions of worldliness; how, in a word, the flesh might be defined as the active principle of the world,[2] and how consequently in these antitheses we find it perpetually contrasted with the spirit, whether the spirit of man, or the personal Holy Spirit of God.

Then, again, when the nature of man is considered simply and by itself, apart from any higher principle, then the contrast is not body and spirit, but body and soul; as when our Lord says, 'Fear not those who

---

[1] See note J. [2] See note K.

can kill the body, but are not able to kill the soul.'[1] Ever the same contrast: when higher principle is balanced against higher principle, then flesh and spirit; when only perishable part against imperishable part, then body and soul. Can these contrasts be merely accidental? Can they be ignored in such an argument? Can they be satisfactorily explained on any other hypothesis than that of a threefold nature, which, when viewed under one aspect, suggests one contrast, and when viewed under another aspect suggests another?

We might almost pause here, and take our stand upon the scripture evidence we have adduced. But in such deeper and more speculative subjects it is never well to close our ears to the voice of antiquity; it is never either prudent or reverent to slight the testimony of the early Church, or to leave unnoticed the antecedent and contemporary opinions of that nation whose sons were the first heralds and preachers of Christianity.

Let us adduce this subsidiary evidence with all brevity, but still not leave it wholly unnoticed.

If we ask, first, whether the Jews recognised any difference between soul and spirit, shall we find any difficulty in answering unhesitatingly in the affirmative? Independent of direct evidence that might be adduced from the Hebrew Scriptures, we meet with traces of this belief in the very Septuagint

---

[1] Matth. x. 28.

translation, in some passages of which the translators have not scrupled to obtrude it, even where in the original there is no direct reference to the subject.[1] We find it, as we might have anticipated, in Philo, repeated in every variety of expression;[2] we find it again in Josephus, who, when he is describing the creation of man, fails not thus to paraphrase the original, 'And God formed man by taking dust out of the ground, and within him he put a soul and a spirit.'[3] We find it, lastly, in the Rabbinical writers, enforced in language of great dogmatical precision, and under modifications,—viz., the addition of a third spiritual principle, the Neshama, or Spirit of God,—which, fairly considered, tend only still more to confirm the antiquity and prevalence of the original dogma.[4]

Passing onward to the earlier writers in the Christian Church, it is easy to show that we find this belief in a tripartite nature, and especially in a difference between soul and spirit, expressed in language of great distinctness and precision. In Irenaeus,[5] the existence and union of body, soul, and spirit is defined as the characteristic and criterion of the perfect man. Justin Martyr speaks of the body as the tenement of the soul, and the soul again as the tenement of the spirit. Clement of Alexandria, amidst much addititious Platonism, is no less definite. Origen, in his commentary on St. John, makes the

[1] See note L.   [2] See note M.   [3] See note N.   [4] See note O.
[5] For the original of this and the following quotations, see note P.

express statement, that the soul is different from the spirit; and in his commentary on the Romans, in a passage quoted by Hammond with distinct approval,[1] he enlarges, not only on this threefold composition of man, but on the relations and interdependence of the component parts. His greatest pupil, Didymus of Alexandria, in his admirable treatise on the Holy Spirit, urges this very text on which we are dwelling as an irrefragable proof of the tripartite nature of man. Gregory of Nyssa, in his special work on man's creation, bases the same truth upon the same text; and, last of all, Basil of Cæsarea defines our imperishable part as soul and spirit, and designates the spirit as that part which bears the truest image of God.

But we must here pause. It might only in conclusion be asked how such a doctrine, thus apparently scriptural, thus supported by some of the profoundest thinkers in the early Church, ever became ignored or disregarded: and it may be answered thus. Two causes tended to its obscuration. *First*, the dangerous ratiocinations of Apollinaris,[2] and his perverted application of this doctrine, threw on it a shade of unmerited suspicion, and caused it to be regarded in the Oriental Church with growing disfavour. *Secondly*, the influence of Tertullian, who opposed it,[3] and still more that of Augustine, who, in his treatise on the

---

[1] See Hammond *on* 1 *Thess. l. c.*   [2] See note Q.
[3] See note R.

soul, even while he theoretically admits it, says that he considers it safer practically to ignore it, so effectually checked its progress in the West, that Gennadius of Marseilles, at the end of the fifth century, conceived himself authorized to denounce the distinction between soul and spirit as contrary to the doctrine of the Church. Its revival in later times is probably due, on the one hand, to the influence of our great English divines, by several of whom—I may name Hammond, Jackson, and Bull[1]—it has been emphatically reasserted; and, on the other hand, to some of the more recent and more candid investigations of the substance of apostolical teaching, which have led even those who affect to speak doubtfully of the philosophical accuracy of the doctrine, frankly to admit its existence in the Apostolic writings, and its reception in the early days of the Gospel.

II. But though we have been compelled to dwell mainly upon the first part of the subject, we cannot leave the second and more practical part wholly unnoticed. If Scripture recognises this distinction between soul and spirit, we would fain ask what it reveals of the peculiar nature of each, what it tells us of their union with the body, and their still more mysterious union with the eternal Spirit of God.

III. Let us recur to the text. We there meet

---

[1] See note S.

with the terms body, soul, and spirit; we have proved that they are the three component parts of man; what further are their natures and relations? Body we know; but what is spirit? what is soul?

Let us endeavour first to arrive at the general Scripture meaning of *spirit*, as from this we can readily deduce the general meaning of *soul*; for as both together make up our incorporeal nature, those portions of it which are not included under the one, will necessarily appertain to the sphere and province of the other. Now are we, on the one hand, to understand by spirit, as used in the text, the Holy Spirit,—the Holy Spirit as far as it dwells in man, the Neshama of the Rabbins, the divine afflatus,[1]— or are we to understand it, on the other hand, as simply denoting the higher portion of our purely human nature, the realm of the powers of the mind, the seat of the conscience, the arbiter of choice, the medium of our cognizance of the divine, that portion, or, if that term be thought to imply too specifically a distinct and separate entity, that side of our immaterial nature which alone admits of association with the Holy Spirit of God? In which of these two senses is it to be taken in the text?

Clearly not in the former: the 'spirit' of the text can never be *per se* the Holy Spirit; the Apostle can never pray that the Holy Spirit may be preserved in his converts in an entire state, preserved complete

---

[1] See note T.

in its proportions,—and this, according to our previous analysis, and according to all principles of scientific grammar, must be the meaning assigned to the words. Surely it is not too much to say,—as Didymus said before on this text,—that such an interpretation almost savours of unintentional blasphemy.[1] An association with the eternal Spirit we may and must admit; the prayer for the entirety of the spirit is but another expression of that great truth; but the simple identity of the spirit mentioned in the text with the Holy Spirit can surely never be maintained. The terms of the prayer would be incongruous, the special use of the pronoun, 'your spirit' (ὑμῶν τὸ πνεῦμα) would be inexplicable, and the plain rule of homogeneity, that the first part should relate to the same subject as the similarly expressed remaining parts, would be distinctly violated. I should scarcely have dwelt upon this opinion if it had not been maintained by so profound a divine as Bishop Bull, and had not been thought to derive some support from the comments of Irenæus and Chrysostom.[2] The language of the former seems certainly somewhat in its favour; but I venture to feel confident that, if we weigh well the few words of Chrysostom, we shall arrive at the conviction that he is not speaking of the Holy Spirit alone, but that he is alluding to the union of our spirit with the Holy Spirit, and that he is but ex-

[1] See extract in note P.   [2] See note U.

pressing this indisputable truth,—that our spirit can only be, and only truly remain whole and complete, when the eternal Spirit dwells within it, and is the Shechinah of that innermost shrine.

The spirit, then, mentioned in the text, must be, as it was ever deemed to be by Gregory of Nyssa, and the early Eastern Church,—the human spirit, the higher side of our incorporeal nature,—the *mind*,[1] as it is termed in Scripture, when contemplated under its intellectual aspects,—the *inner man*,[2] as it is also denoted, when viewed in its purely theologicalrelations, in a word, the moving, ruling, and animating principle of our nature. And by its completeness and integrity, that for which the Apostle so fervently prayed, what else can he mean than its permanent, enduring, yea, and indissoluble union with the eternal Spirit of God, without which the spirit of man becomes only a warring chaos of mere intellectual forces, a region of darkness and death?

If there is any one point of more practical importance than another in this mysterious subject, it is the recognition of this vital truth, that it is the spirit which is the medium of communication with the eternal Spirit, and that it is the spirit more especially, in which or with which the Holy Ghost has vouchsafed to dwell. I will confirm this by two texts. *First*, when St. Paul tells us, in his Epistle to the Romans, that 'the Spirit beareth witness to our

---

[1] Eph. iv. 17; Tit. i. 15, al.   [2] Rom. vii. 22; Eph. iii. 16.

spirit that we are the sons of God,[1] what other inference can we draw than this,—that the spirit is that exalted portion of our nature which is the medium of our communication with the sanctifying Spirit of God? And *secondly*, when the same Apostle, in his Epistle to the Ephesians, exhorts his converts to be renewed 'by the Spirit of the mind'[2]—for such is the accurate translation—can we understand aright, or can we adequately explain these elliptical words, unless with Chrysostom,—and I might here add Bishop Bull,—we interpret them to mean the Holy Spirit, which is the inmate of the mind,—the Holy Spirit, that dwells in the higher part of man, and makes man's spirit his tabernacle?[3]

Thus, then, the spirit is the higher power within us, the medium of our communication with, and the very temple of the Holy Ghost; and its completeness consists in its union with that blessed Spirit, both here and hereafter.

A few words on the nature of the *soul*, its relation to the spirit, and its condition of integrity, and our imperfect investigation must conclude.

As I before said, a knowledge of the term spirit almost implies that of soul. If the spirit be the higher and ruling side of our incorporeal nature, the soul must be the lower side, and the subject of the spirit's sway. But observe, brethren, we should

---

[1] Ch. viii. 16.   [2] Ch. iv. 23.   [3] See notes and reff. *in loc.*

never exhaust the scriptural meaning of the term soul, if we failed to admit that Scripture often represents it to us as almost necessarily involving and including the spirit, as, in a word, being that which constitutes and makes up the true personality. It is thus that Scripture never speaks of the salvation of the spirit, but the salvation of the *soul;* it is thus that the term soul becomes almost synonymous with that of *heart*, and points to that assemblage of feelings, movements, and impulses, of which the heart is the imaginary tabernacle.[1] It is thus that it is represented to us as poised, as it were, between the powers of the seen, and the powers of the unseen world, swayed to and fro between the flesh and the spirit,—borne hither, borne thither, with the tide of their conflict, or standing the irresolute, yet not unmoved spectatress, of that fell and fearful strife. O well, indeed, might the Apostle, he who had felt all this within his own bosom, put up a prayer for every convert and saint of Thessalonica, that his soul,—itself the very arena, as well as the prize of that fearful strife,—might be preserved entire unto the coming of the Lord. And in what can that wholeness and entirety consist, save in its more complete union, by the medium of its higher congener, with the quickening spirit of God; and, still more by its preservation, through Him who took flesh to save it,—from all that works spiritual deterioration and decay,—from the corrup-

---

[1] See notes on 1 *Tim.* i. 5.

tion of earth-born affections, the disintegrating powers of wilder passions, the disruptive force of lawless instincts, the gnawing tooth of baser cravings, the corrosion of lower cares, the fretting moth of earthliness, the rust of the world, and the canker of the flesh? Even so does the wholeness and entirety of the body—a profound and mysterious subject, to which we can now only thus briefly advert—depend on the preservation of the outward fabric from the material corruption engendered by the lower appetites of the flesh, the physical depravations of self-indulgence, intemperance, carnalities, and lust.

We often speak lightly of such things, yet all tend to the untimely demolition of the outward tabernacle; all help to efface from the brow the image and lineaments of its Maker; all help to stamp thereon the visible image of Satan,—that image round which, traced as with the finger of death, for ever runs this legend and superscription, HE THAT SOWETH TO THE FLESH, SHALL OF THE FLESH REAP CORRUPTION.[1]

Finally then, to sum up all, let us say that our text has led us to these conclusions:— that body, soul, and spirit are the three component parts of man's nature. That the spirit may be regarded more as the realm of the intellectual forces, and the shrine of the Holy Ghost. That the soul may be regarded more as the region of the feelings, affections, and

[1] Gal. vi. 8.

impulses, of all that peculiarly individualizes and personifies. Lastly, that these three parts, especially the two incorporeal elements, are intimately associated and united, and form the media of communication, both with each other, and with the higher and the lower elements. So that thus we may put before our thoughts these five things,—the phenomenal world, the body, the soul, the spirit, and the invisible kingdom of God, and may say,—that as the body is the medium of communication between the soul and the phenomenal world, so the soul is the medium of communication between the body and the spirit, and the spirit the medium between the soul and the Holy Spirit of God.

But let us not for one moment dream that subjects so deep, relations so mysterious, and interdependences so implicit, can be summed up in a single formula, or included in a single enunciation. In this hasty survey, we have left very many points of interest wholly unnoticed. We have discussed none of those passages in which soul and spirit are used with greater amplitude, and in which the one term is clearly understood to include the other; we have not analysed their seeming interchanges, nor fully traced out their more than seeming distinctions. All we have done is to trace out a few outlines, and to lay down a few elementary definitions. Nevertheless, it is my humble conviction, that these outlines are not untruly drawn. Nay I would dare to say, that if any of you should feel induced to carry out these thoughts for yourselves, and to supply what is deficient, you would perchance not only obtain a deeper insight into the peculiar language of Scripture, but also appreciate more fully the esssential character of those temptations that try alike body, soul, and spirit, that loosen the bands of the compound nature, and destroy the entirety of its constituent parts.

May these feeble words have wrought in you an increased conviction, that deep indeed is the mystery of our humanity, and dreadful our responsibility, if, with such marvellous elements of our being, with principles thus fearfully and thus wonderfully combined, and a composite nature thus mysteriously perfect, we yield them to the service of their destroyers, the world, the flesh, and the devil,—the threefold league against our threefold nature. May these words humbly serve to have quickened us all to dedicate all parts of our being, individually and collectively, to that triune God, who fashioned the body, who redeems the soul, and who sanctifies the spirit:—that so, when the hour of earthly disunion takes place, when dust returns to dust, and soul and spirit depart unto God, we may, with a humble trustfulness and hope, commit ourselves to our Creator, and await the hour when the mortal shall put on immortality, and all shall be again united in holiness, purity, and incorruption.

SERMON VI.

THE COMMUNION OF SAINTS.

Rev. xiv. 13.

And I heard a voice from heaven saying unto me, Write, Blessed are the dead which die in the Lord from henceforth: Yea, saith the Spirit, that they may rest from their labours; and their works do follow them.

THIS, brethren, is the special day in our Academic year in which we are more particularly called upon by the service[1] in which we are about to share, to meditate upon lofty and elevating themes, and doctrines of grave and mysterious import. On this day, we, the living members of this ancient University, commemorate the bounty of those wise, and good, and holy men who have helped to make us what we are,—who have laid the foundation-stones of our institutions, and have built them up with their love, and their bounty, and their prayers. On such a day, it seems impossible to repress the yearning of our spirits to realize in some measure the nature of our spiritual union with those whom we

---

[1] The Commemoration of Benefactors.

so gratefully and lovingly commemorate,—it seems almost unnatural to check the desire to dwell upon the mystical bond that unites us with the holy dead, and to meditate upon the more special applications of the doctrine of the communion of saints.

On such a day, then, I make no apology for directing your meditations to these more mysterious, yet most consolatory aspects of our faith; nay, I should feel that I had failed to perform the duty allotted to me, if I were to pass over, with an unsympathizing reserve, the solemn subjects which the services of the day bring before us. Cold, indeed, would it be, on such an occasion, to make no allusion to doctrines that ever lie near the heart of every thinking man, and that in hours of sadder musings, in afflictions, and bereavement, and desolation, are perchance the only fountains of comfort, the only ministers of hope, when all around seems hopelessness and despair. I feel, indeed, that we are venturing upon grave topics round which many a cloud of uncertainty still lingers,—I feel that we must pass over ground on which the dust of controversy is not yet laid, that we must consider doubtful questions, and endeavour to adjust mysterious relations;—still we shall be wise to dare all, rather than lend ourselves to the melancholy realism of the present day, that never regards itself more judicious than when it practically denies all the vital truths which emanate from the doctrine of the communion of saints, and avows its indifference to the lofty consolations that may be derived from the commemoration of the holy dead.

It may be not wholly uninteresting or unprofitable to pause briefly to consider, to what tendencies, and to what developments of modern thought, we can reasonably ascribe this practical disregard of what is at the same time both so edifying and so consolatory. To what are we to ascribe the present open disregard of the doctrine of the communion of saints? Apparently to the influence of two opposing forms of error, both of which root themselves in the modern views entertained in reference to death, and what lies beyond it. On the one hand, we have a melancholy *Sadduceeism*, that seems to regard it almost a point of religious duty to dismiss all considerations respecting our brethren that sleep,—a Sadduceeism that thrusts its dead hastily out of sight, that ignores their examples, that disowns association with them, that practically regards death as the end of all things, and the grave a chasm between the visible and invisible Church too wide to allow even thought to overleap. On the other hand, we may everywhere recognise a buoyant and ardent theosophy, that sees in the future only a purer and sublimated present,— a future in which activities will be more persistent, energies more concentrated, fields of labour and duty more inviting and more expanded; that regards life as an antepast,—death a natural process of purification, a prescribed mode of riddance from earthly and material elements, and the grave a meet place wherein to deposit the cast-off weeds of an obstructive and cumbersome humanity.[1]

Now I shall not on the present occasion attempt a confutation of either of these views, I will not even pause to show how they involve the gravest misconceptions of the cardinal doctrines of Christianity; how the tendency of the one is to a dreary isolation and materialism, of the other to an almost more repulsive spirituality: I allude to them only as both truly existing in the present day, and as both so seriously at variance with the consolations that flow from the doctrine of the communion of saints, as to cause it, if not at present to be openly denied, yet to be practically disregarded. With the one of these views, the communion of saints, if it mean anything at all, is either wholly removed to another sphere of existence, or is deemed little more than a community in religious prejudice, an acknowledgment of a partial and sectarian union. With the other, it implies little more than the belief in a future reunion of persons and interests under more auspicious circumstances, and with fewer elements of impediment and change than in the present state of things. The one, in fact, is the creed of a selfish and often hopeless Christianity, the other the creed of an aspiring and hopeful paganism. Both differ gravely, in all their ultimate tendencies, from the truth, and from one another; both, however, have some points of union,

---

[1] See Sermon IV. p 55.

both some common forms of opposition to catholic truth. These points of union may, perhaps, ultimately be reduced to *two*,—a direct or practical denial of the existence of any intermediate state, and, as a consequence of it,—the denial of any real existing relations between us who linger here and our brethren who have passed within the vail.

And here two lines of argument present themselves: either we may endeavour to substantiate the existence of an intermediate state, and then deduce the relations that subsist between the living and the departed, or, on the other hand, we may endeavour to show that there are real and true relations between the members of the visible and invisible Church, and leave the considerations of the exact state to follow in the way of natural consequence.

The latter course of argument is perhaps most edifying, and most in harmony with the present occasion.

Let us endeavour, then, to take up that portion of the doctrine of the communion of saints which treats more especially of the actual relations between the faithful who are on earth, and the faithful who have departed,—that portion of the subject which has been somewhat briefly dismissed by Bishop Pearson,[1] as involving perplexing relations, but which, I still venture to think, in these latter days of materialism and incredulity, is of the highest practical importance.

---

[1] See note A.

Let us investigate these relations calmly and dispassionately, and, proceeding from more obvious and general conditions of communion, prepare ourselves briefly to consider the more specific relations which the services of the day suggest, and in which the chief interest of these speculations has always appeared to reside.

To begin, then; there is, in the first place, clearly a communion between the saints on earth and the saints that have entered their rest, based on the relation of *Love*. This was the foundation of all the touching commemorations that we find in the ancient Liturgies.[1] In those days of a more real and stirring devotion, the dead in Christ were not forgotten, the unity of the Church was a living and vital truth. Those who were still tarrying on earth for their Lord's coming would not, and could not believe themselves separated from those whom they had loved on earth, who had joined in the same prayers, who had knelt at the same altar, who had broken the same bread, who had become members of the same mystical body. Where were *they* now whom they had so loved and so reverenced? the holy, and the just, and the true; they who had been bound to them by such hallowed ties; who with them had so earnestly and so longingly awaited the Lord's coming, who had spread abroad His word,—who had shared His cross, —who had so eagerly sought to fill up the mystical

---

[1] See note E.

measure of His sufferings,[1] and who had fallen on sleep before all was accomplished. Where were they now? Were they lying in dull unbroken slumber, wrapt in unconsciousness, and darkness, and oblivion?[2] Or were they far, far distant, in unknown realms, pursuing with all the energy and intensity of purely spiritual natures mysterious missions, which were ever carrying them farther and farther from those with whom they once had so bravely toiled and suffered, and with whom they had borne the heat and burden of the outworn day? Ah! no; the heart revolted against such an unsympathizing theology; the spirit within bare witness against it. The ancient Church felt and knew that its true members were all united,—whether in life or death, inseparable,—whether on earth or in Paradise, all one. It could not, and would not, forget them. It felt that, though absent in flesh, they were nigh, very nigh in spirit, praising with them the same Lord, praying with them for the hastening of His kingdom.

Verily *Love* was the corner-stone of the doctrine of the communion of the Saints.

Again, the communion between the holy living and the holy dead exists in the common relation of *Faith*. Could they, who had been sharers in that vital element, who together had realized that substance of things hoped for,[3] that evidence of things not seen, be dissociated either in life or in death? What is

---

[1] Col. i 24.   [2] See note C.   [3] Heb. xi. 1.

there in the deposition and divestiture of these earthly elements that can affect a union based on the participation in a common spiritual principle, which the everlasting word of God teaches us is the sole condition of vitality,—which an Apostle has declared, out of the depth of his own personal experiences, as the sole instrument and medium of all true life, whether in the flesh or in the spirit? Relations may be changed, degrees altered; the faith of the pilgrim in the flesh may be less constant and vivid than in the unclothed spirit, that sees with an inward eye along a brighter perspective, where earthborn mist and vapour can neither becloud nor obscure. What now appears indistinct and incoherent may then be found clear in outline, and faultless in symmetry; what seems now but as the mirage, may then be descried as the solid towers and battlements of the city of God. The very passage from the world of sense to the world of spirits may involve heightened conditions of belief, a purer and more sublimated faith. Changes there may be; development we may expect; but till faith cease in the fulness of fruition, till we all be for ever and for ever with Him, in whom we have hoped and believed, faith will not cease to be an ever-living bond that connects the holy living and the holy dead, a bond that time cannot weaken, or death destroy, but that remains vital, energizing, and indissoluble.

Scarcely one of the ancient liturgies leaves this holy bond unnoticed, or fails, directly or indirectly, to ground its commemoration of the departed on this common principle of union and life. Thus it is that, in the venerable Oriental liturgy that tradition has ascribed to St. Basil,[1] the Church militant calls upon God to be mindful of the departed, who have professed *the right word of faith*. Thus it is that, in the ancient liturgy of Constantinople, the early Christians specially offered unto God *their reasonable service for those who rested in faith*. In faith all were united, all of the same fraternal band; living servants of the same living Lord, members of the same body, branches of the same vine.

Thirdly, there is the blessed union of *Hope*. In this the waiting and longing servant of the Lord was one with those who had approached to realization, but who had not yet received the crown. In hope, the Church on earth was tarrying and praying; in hope, the Church in Paradise was awaiting its consummation of bliss. Hope bound both together in a living unity; in hope was the salvation of the living; in hope the blessedness of the dead. Hope and Faith were the notes of the Church of the first-born. Nor is it without a deep significance, that the Apostle St. John has put most prominently forward amid those who were bound together in the mournful companionship of woe and perdition, those in whom these vital principles had no place. To the *fearful* and to the *unbelieving*, no less than to the murderer and

---

[1] See note D.

the sorcerer, is meted out the bitter portion of the burning lake, and the dread issues of the irreversible sentence.[1]

But may we proceed further? Have we any scriptural grounds for asserting a yet more intimate communion,—a communion not merely consisting in the participation in common elements of life, but in common acts of adoration? Is there any trace of a yet more mysterious bond, the bond of united supplication, thanksgiving, and prayer? . . . . . Let us be cautious; let us be circumspect; let us beware of intruding with a fleshly mind into what we see not. Yet let us not from a false timidity or polemical scrupulosity, be too ready to give up all the adorable consolations which the word of God and the services of our Church seem so fully to minister.

Prayer, in its most inclusive form, has three principal aspects. It is *eucharistic*, in which we may include the service of praise; it is *supplicatory*; it is *intercessory*. Have we communion in all, or in any of these, with the faithful departed? When our blended voices rise up to God, are there portions of our prayers in which those who once joined with us may be united with us still; or is it true, in the most sternly literal sense of the words, that the living, the living alone, can praise and glorify the living God?[2]

Let us consider briefly the service of *Praise*. Can

---

[1] Rev. xxi. 8.   [2] Isaiah xxxviii. 19.

we doubt that in this there must still be a union of a very real and vital nature? When, in that noble hymn in our morning service, alike laudatory and commemorative, we declare that the glorious company of the Apostles, the goodly fellowship of the prophets, the noble army of martyrs, and the holy Church throughout all the world, *praise the Lord,*—are we uttering mere unmeaning words? Are we using language merely figurative and symbolical? If we know that in some portions of our service of praise we use words with which angels glorify their Creator, yea, if we are sure that we are permitted to utter accents that day and night are sounding in the courts of heaven, which the most transcendent order of created beings,—the mystic Four that surround the eternal throne, are pouring forth in ceaseless adoration;—if we are one with angels, and archangels, and all the company of heaven, in ascribing praise and honour to Him that was, and is, and is to come,[1] can the holy dead be silent in that universal hymn? Amid those prayers that mingled with the incense before the throne,—those prayers that the rapt Evangelist was specially moved to record as *the prayers of all saints,*[2] are the praises and prayers of the saintly departed alone wanting? Is the sting of death so sharp, has the grave such victory? It cannot be. Though we may not define in what measure, in what place, or with what precise circumstances of

---

[1] Rev. iv. 8.   [2] Rev. viii. 3.

union, yet it surely does not seem a rash dream to imagine that when our voices rise up to God in united praise and adoration, there may be other voices that we hear not rising to heaven simultaneously with ours, there may be others that we see not bowing down in not unlike homage before the Lord of Sabaoth, and adoring the Universal King.[1]

May we advance a step further? Can there be any union in worship in its *supplicatory* form? Are there any prayers in which we and those who have departed can have any participation? Is there a communion so close and living as this? We do not seem justified in speaking with confidence. Yet there are mysterious notices in the last revelation of God to man, that would lead us to believe that there are prayers and aspirations that are and must be common to the universal Church of Christ. When we stand by the grave of a departed brother, and pray the Lord that He would shortly accomplish the number of His elect, and hasten His kingdom,—when in our daily services we use our Master's words, and pray that *His kingdom may come*, are there no echoes of any sympathizing prayer from those who have ceased to belong to the Church on earth? Was there not one at least who was permitted to hear the passionate tones of a strangely accordant supplication? ' And I saw under the altar the souls of them that were

---

[1] See note E.

slain for the word of God, and for the testimony which they held: and they cried with a loud voice, saying, How long, O Lord, holy and true, dost thou not judge and avenge our blood on them that dwell on the earth?'[1]

Though it can never be wise to press unduly such mysterious revelations, yet surely it is not presumptuous to entertain the belief that there *are* prayers which so wholly transcend all earthly conditions, all relations of the visible and material,—prayers so mysteriously comprehensive, that in them both the visible and invisible Church may join in one mingled voice of supplication. And that voice shall not die out into silence till all be fulfilled, and until He that cometh hath come, and no more doth tarry.

Are we justified in taking one step yet further? We have seen that it is probable that there is a communion of praise between the visible and invisible Church. We have seen that it is not improbable that there may be certain forms of supplication in which both may share. Have we scriptural authority for asserting, or just grounds for believing, that in the third form of prayer, the *intercessory*, both may still further be participators; that they may pray for us who are still fighting the good fight, and we for them who have fought it out to the end, but to whom the last day has not yet brought its crown and its consummated felicities? Let us spend a few closing

---

[1] Rev. vi. 9, 10.

thoughts on the probabilities or possibilities of such a supposition.

First, have we reasons from Scripture for thinking that the holy dead pray *for us;* and, if Scripture is silent, does such a supposition prepare the way for deductions inconsistent with any of the fundamental principles of our Faith? The answer is short: Scripture *does not* supply us with any just and certain grounds for concluding that the holy dead pray for the living. Scripture hints, indeed, more than once, as in the case of the rich man in the parable and his surviving brethren,[1] at the existence of an enduring *sympathy* between the living and the dead. It leaves us indeed, not without the deep consciousness that the faithful departed who loved us on earth, love us still—love us ever; yea, I know not that it condemns the thought that their love may in some way evince itself in actions; that gentle footsteps may be near us waiting with unseen ministries; that loved faces, cleansed from the dishonours of the grave, may be gazing on us with an immortal sympathy which may reach into the inner depths of our spiritual nature, and console, and strengthen, and quicken.[2] But farther than these irrepressible suggestions of love we know not; and we may fervently bless God for the veil he has so mercifully interposed. We may adore His mercy, that He has saved us from the inevitable snare that would have attended the actual

---

[1] Luke xvi. 27, 28. [2] See note F.

knowledge of any intercessory functions on the part of the members of the invisible Church. It would be almost impossible to resist aspirations that these purer prayers might ascend to God for us. And aspirations would lead to entreaties, and entreaties to prayers; and at last we should find ourselves on the brink of that frightful form of error, that dares to multiply mediators,—that debases itself lower than the angel-worshippers of Colossæ,—that wearies the holy dead with invocations which startle their very repose in Paradise,—yea, that only fill them with a still more passionate longing for the hour, when all that tends to derogate from their Master's glories and from the efficacy of His all-sufficient sacrifice, *all that loveth and maketh a lie*[1] shall be judged with the judgment of the second death.

Again, on the other side, can we pray *for them?* Does Scripture suggest or authorize such a fervent expression of the intensity of our hope and our love? Can we on the one hand dare to say confidently, *yes?* Are we prepared, on the other, to say that those most ancient prayers for the refreshment of the saints that sleep, their merciful judgment, and their consummation of felicity,—prayers that have found a place in every early liturgy of the world, and are to some extent echoed in our prayer for the Church militant,—are fondly and vainly devised? Are we so hasty as to denounce the guarded expression of prayerful

---

[1] Rev. xxii. 15.

hope that will form a part of this day's service? I trust not. Let us treat the question calmly and dispassionately. Scripture is for the most part silent. It certainly does not enjoin it preceptively, for in the passage that bids us pray for all men,[1] the specifications which follow peculiarly limit the intercessions to the cases of the *living*. Nor can we confidently say that it suggests it by way of example; for though St. Paul's prayer for Onesiphorus does not unnaturally bear that construction,[2] yet to found positively a doctrine, on the supposition that the preceding words 'the household of Onesiphorus' imply that the master of it was no more, seems in the highest degree unwise and precarious. Scripture is silent; yet antiquity plainly speaks. How then are we to decide? What opinion are we to form on this immemorial practice of the ancient Church?

Perhaps the following observations will lead us to some sort of general decision.

First, no calm student of antiquity can fail to observe, that the practice of praying for the dead had ever a distinct tendency to dangerous progressions and developments. We first meet with commemorations in which *communion in faith* was the thing mainly dwelt upon, and the blessed and salutary teaching of example the end mainly proposed. We next meet with distinct intercessory prayers, yet

---

[1] 1 Tim. ii. 1. [2] See note G.

only for the holy dead, and in language of restrained and edifying simplicity. A step onward leads us to compassionate extensions of prayer for those whose state is doubtful; a step further, and we observe a lapse into prayers even for the reprobate, and we begin to meet with melancholy ideas of short-lived consolations that it was possible to supply to those in anticipatory torment.[1] We soon hear the not unreasonable protests of Aerius;[2] and we find ourselves, amid doubtful language even from Catholic Fathers, drifting into morbid hopes and self-interested superstitions; and at last silently, yet surely, borne onward into the resuscitated paganism of Purgatory, and into all the frightful abuses which that perverted doctrine imported into the Church of Christ.

Secondly, we cannot fail to observe, that prayers for the dead lose much of their propriety, if not their efficacy, from our ignorance of the *exact* state of the departed. Though we may wisely adopt the ancient and Catholic belief, that the holy dead are in a place of great peace and blessedness, hopefully awaiting their final consummation of bliss, and their portion in the first resurrection; and that the unholy dead, in some silent abodes of misery and darkness, are despairingly awaiting the issues of the judgment, and the accomplishment of the final sentence;— though we may adopt such a belief with some degree

---

[1] See note II.   [2] See note I.

of confidence, yet still, even thus, our knowledge is far too limited to allow us in our public services to adopt any other language than that of the most generic supplication, and the most cautious and guarded prayer. To approach the throne of grace with supplications in behalf of what is unknown, uncertain, or irreversible, is fearfully to offend the eternal majesty of God, and to do daring violence to the true nature and essence of prayer.

These two considerations,—*first*, the tendency of reciprocal intercession to develop itself into two fatal and destructive forms of error, worship of the creature on this side, and purgatory or universalism on that; and *secondly*, our real ignorance of the state of those for whom we would fain pray,—may lead us finally to the conclusion, that the reformed Church of England, in its second Prayer-book, showed its wisdom in silently removing from its regular and general services prayers, that, by no necessary connexion, but by the gradual corruption of the times, had become associated with perilous error.[1] And yet again, the antiquity and universality of such prayers may lead us also consistently to acknowledge, that our Church further showed its wisdom in not specifically *condemning* them, and in not definitely forbidding expressions of prayerful *hope*, which, under peculiar circumstances, and under the most jealous and rigid limitations, it might seem permissible to offer to

---

[1] See note J.

the Lord of the living and the dead.[1] Communion, however, in such prayer, cannot be asserted. For if it seem more than probable that there is only the existence of a loving *sympathy* for us on their side, and if it be most dangerous to breathe any other accents than those of *hope* for them on ours,—then all real communion in intercessory supplications, all that true reciprocity which is the real essence of such forms of prayer, must be considered even more than doubtful or precarious.

And now we have brought our meditations to their natural close. We have seen, I trust, that the communion of the visible and invisible Church is something real, vital, and practical. That it is a communion in love, a communion in faith, a communion in hope, yea, and a communion in prayer, both in its laudatory and supplicatory, though *not* in its intercessory form; still, that the faithful here and the faithful in Paradise are one, united, and inseparable, and that against such a union the grave has no power, and the bitterness of death is unprevailing.

Wherefore, with comforted and quickened hearts, let us join in the pious services of this holy day; let us gratefully and lovingly commemorate aloud the wise and the munificent, the pure and the saintly, those who are joined to us by the near ties of bounty and love; yea, and with them let us commemorate in spirit all the company of saints,—the martyrs,

---

[1] See note K.

confessors, bishops, presbyters, and all the faithful servants of God, whether in the schools, the courts, or the camp, that have belonged to our mother University,—all that noble spiritual ancestry, which every true-hearted man among us can so proudly and so joyfully claim as his own. Here have dwelt, and here have toiled, the holy and the saintly, the faithful and the self-denying, the wise and the good. Of many the memories are fresh among us. We can point to the homes where they dwelt, the cloisters which they paced, the altars at which they worshipped: their words are yet sounding in our ears: of some the well-remembered image has not yet faded away from our inward eye. And in spirit they are with us still; they mark our efforts to glorify God in our appointed offices and callings; they quicken us with their sympathies; they rejoice in our unity; they mourn when divided counsels separate us, or when a rash spirit of innovation, or a timid obstructiveness, seeks to mar the usefulness of those noble foundations which they laid with such wisdom, such bounty, and such love. Can we reject such sympathy; can we remain dead and cold to such a holy and quickening communion?

No! verily; let us live as if they were still with us in the flesh; let us walk worthy of such a lineage, while here on earth; and let us make ourselves meet to enjoy the fulness of communion with them hereafter. Oh, let us bless God for their examples; let us pray to Him for strength to emulate their self-denial, for grace to follow after their meek wisdom, for courage patiently and hopefully to labour in the service of God, even as they laboured,—to live as they lived, and to die as they died. And then, when we too are called to our God; when the pilgrimage of life is over; when the heat and burden of the day have been bravely borne; when the watching eyes are closing in slumber, and the weary head is at rest, may we pass into their blessed company, and with them in hope and bliss await the hour for which the angels are longing, and the Church praying, and all material creation groaning and travailing,[1]—the hour when the mystical number of the elect shall be completed, the hundred and forty and four thousand sealed, and the kingdoms of the world become the kingdoms of Christ. 'And I heard a great voice out of heaven saying, Behold, the tabernacle of God is with men, and He will dwell with them, and they shall be His people, and God Himself shall be with them, and be their God.'[2]

---

[1] Rom. viii. 22; see Sermon I.   [2] Rev. xxi. 3.

NOTES.

SERMON I.

Note A, p. 2.

This is shown very distinctly by the fact that Usteri, in the last two editions of his *Entwick. d. Paulin. Lehrb.* p. 379 sq. (ed. 5), has seen it right to retract the opinion advanced in the first three editions that κτίσις (on the interpretation of which all turns) was to be limited to *mankind*. The opinions of the modern commentators, Tholuck, Reiche, Rückert, Olshausen, Fritzsche, De Wette, Philippi, Meyer, Alford, will all be found *substantially* accordant. Some, as Olshausen, stretch the reference of κτίσις somewhat too wide ('the totality of all creation, οὐρανὸς καὶ γῆ, the spiritual and material world'); others, again, as Fritzsche, as unduly limit it merely to inanimate creation ('ipsam mundi machinam; cœlos, sidera, aerem, terram'); still the substantial accordance is sufficiently striking to give the inquirer considerable confidence in the general outlines of the interpretation proposed by modern commentators. The most satisfactory view of κτίσις seems that advanced at p. 4, with which that of Meyer ('die gesammte vernunftlose Schöpfung, lebendig und leblos'), and De Wette ('die ganze leblose und lebendige Natur im Gegensatze gegen die Menscheit') is most nearly coincident. The reader, who is anxious to enter into the details of this profound text, will find, in addition to the commentaries above mentioned, a good sermon by Delitzsch, *Bibl. Psychol.* p. 419, and a careful article by Rupprecht in the *Stud. u. Kritik.* for 1851, p. 214—236, in answer to opinions advanced by Zyro in a former number (1845. Part II.). Some curious thoughts will be found in an article entitled 'Die seufzende Creatur,' by Von Meyer, *Blätter für Höh. Wahrh.* Vol. vi. p. 334, and still more so in the singular but noticeable treatise by the Genevese Philosopher, Bonnet, *La Palingénésie Philosophique*, Vol. i. p. 169 sq.

Note B, p. 2.

The early Church seems to have interpreted this passage substantially in accordance with the views alluded to in the preceding note. We may make the following extracts; Irenæus, *contr. Hær.* v. 32, p. 331 (ed. Mass.), 'Dives in omnibus Deus, et omnia sunt ejus. Oportet ergo et ipsam conditionem, reintegratam ad pristinum, sine prohibitione servire justis : et hoc Apostolus fecit manifestum in eâ quæ est ad Romanos, sic dicens : '*Nam expectatio creaturæ*, &c.' (see also cap. 33, ad fin.) ;—Chrysostom, *in Rom. l. c.* Vol. ix. p. 641 (ed. Bened. 1837), ὥστε δὲ ἐμφαντικώτερον γενέσθαι τὸν λόγον καὶ προσωποποιεῖ τὸν κόσμον ἅπαντα τοῦτον ; in p. 643, we find the κτίσις further defined as διὰ σὲ [ἄνθρωπον] πάντα γινομένη, and distinguished from man as devoid of reason, εἰ γὰρ ἡ κτίσις τοῦτο ποιεῖ, πολλῷ μᾶλλον σὲ δίκαιον τοῦτο ἐπιδείκνυσθαι τὸν λόγῳ τετιμημένον ;—Theodoret, *in loc.*. Vol. iii. p. 88 (ed. Schulze), διδάσκει δὲ, ὡς πᾶσα ἡ κτίσις ἡ ὁρωμένη, θνητὴν ἔλαχε φύσιν ;—Cyrill. in Cramer, *Caten.* p. 134, 246, καὶ αὐτὴ πάντως ἡ κτίσις μεθαρμοσθήσεται πρὸς τὸ ἄμεινον, τὴν πρέπουσαν τοῖς τότε καιροῖς αὐχοῦσα κατάστασιν. Καὶ πρός γε τοῦτο ἡμᾶς ὁ θεσπέσιος Πέτρος ἐνδοιάζειν οὐκ ἐᾷ, εἰπὼν ὅτι καινοὺς οὐρανοὺς καὶ καινὴν γῆν κατὰ τὰ ἐπαγγέλματα αὐτοῦ προσδοκῶμεν ;—Origen, *in loc.* (Vol. vii. p. 98, ed. Lomm), and more decidedly, *de Princip.* i. 7 (Vol. xxi. p. 120, ed.

Lomm), seems to refer the κτίσις to what has been invested with a material and corruptible bodily substance; but the interpretation is evidently somewhat subordinated to preconceived speculations on the corruptibility of the corporeal; comp. Tertull. *adv. Hermog.* cap. 11. The list of patristic references could be much increased, but enough perhaps has been adduced generally to justify the assertion to which the note refers.

Note C, p. 4.

By the term 'widest application' I do not intend to imply one so wide as that urged by Olshausen (see note A), but, merely the widest that is in any way compatible with the terms of the revelation. For the substantially accordant views of the Greek Fathers on κτίσις, see the quotations in the preceding note. The Latin Fathers appear to have been less uniform in their interpretation. With the opinion of Augustine cited below, contrast that of Ambrose (*Epist.* xxxiv. Vol. iii. p. 1076, ed. Migne), who appears to extend the reference of κτίσις to the heavenly bodies, and that of Gregory (*Moral. in Job*, xxxiv. 18, Vol. i. p. 675, ed. Migne), who appears to restrict it to mankind. It is, however, not always easy to elicit the exact and definite opinion of the patristic writers on special texts, except in their commentaries; as they not uncommonly, in their general treatises, refer to passages as illustrating, without necessarily precisely coinciding with, the opinions they are at the time advancing. Of modern writers, Bishop Jeremy Taylor is often similarly varied in his application of the same texts: in one treatise, for example, we may find one view taken of a debated passage, clearly and decidedly; in another treatise we may find a very different view, and without any hint of a change of opinion.

Note D, p. 4.

The exact words of Augustine are as follows : ' Quod autem ait, *Nam expectatio creaturæ, etc.*, usque ad id quod ait, *et ipse, etc.*, sic intelligendum est, ut neque sensum dolendi et gemendi opinemur esse in arboribus et oleribus et lapidibus, et cæteris hujuscemodi creaturis ; *hic enim error Manichæorum est:* neque Angelos sanctos vanitati subjectos esse arbitremur, et de his existimemus quod liberabuntur a servitute interitus, cum interituri utique non sint ; sed omnem creaturam in ipso homine sine ullâ calumniâ cogitemus.'—*Prop. ex Ep. ad Rom.*, 53, Vol. iii. p. 2074 (ed. Migne).

Note E, p. 4.

The Greek Fathers, *e. g.* Chrysostom, *in loc.*, and Gregory, cited by Cramer (*Caten. in Rom.* p. 246), appear to have felt no difficulty in the prosopopœia. The words of the former are very much to the point ; ὥστε δὲ ἐμφαντικώτερον γενέσθαι τὸν λόγον καὶ προσωποποιεῖ τὸν κόσμον ἅπαντα τοῦτον· ἅπερ καὶ οἱ προφῆται ποιοῦσιν, ποταμοὺς κροτοῦντας χερσὶν εἰσάγοντες, καὶ βουνοὺς ἁλλομένους, καὶ τὰ ὄρη σκιρτῶντα· οὐχ ἵνα ταῦτα ἔμψυχα εἶναι νομίσωμεν, οὐδ᾽ ἵνα λογισμόν τινα ζῶμεν αὐτοῖς, ἀλλ᾽ ἵνα τὴν ὑπερβολὴν μάθωμεν τῶν ἀγαθῶν, ὡς καὶ τῶν ἀναισθήτων αὐτῶν καθικνουμένην. Modern poetry has expressed itself in terms still more decided :

> Es geht ein allgemeines Weinen,
> So weit die stille Sterne scheinen,
> Durch alle Adern der Natur ;
> Es ringt und seufzt nach der Verklärung,
> Entgegenschmachtend der Gewährung
> In Liebesangst die Creatur.
>
> *Fr. von Schlegel.*

Note F, p. 6.

'Dicitur Deus ὁ ὑποτάξας summus omnium rerum moderator (Rom. xi. 36), et quem terram exsecratum esse Genesis diserte testetur, iii. 17, v. 29,' Fritzsche *in loc.;* so also De Wette and Meyer. The early Greek commentators are not coincident in their views; Chrysostom refers it generally to man (διὰ σὲ τὸν ἄνθρωπον), Theodoret, more correctly, to the ὅρον τοῦ δημιουργήσαντος: so also (of the Latin writers) Ambrose, who (*Epist.* xxxiv.) distinctly refers it to the 'divinum arbitrium.'

Note G, p. 7.

The derivation of ματαιότης is not perfectly certain. The most probable opinion, however, is that the word stands in philological affinity with ΜΑΩ, ματεύω; comp. Pott, *Etym. Forsch.* Vol. i. p. 242, but see also p. 8.

Note H, p. 8.

It is to be lamented that a man so favourably known to the scientific world as the late Professor Oersted should have expressed almost undisguised contempt for opinions which, as he himself admits, were conceived to rest on the authority of St. Paul: 'Neither Christ nor any of the biblical writers who benefited by his oral instruction [had St. Paul no special and personal revelations, 2 Cor. xii. 7 ?] have mentioned the corruption of nature by the fall. When we therefore refer to the Bible we must rely on St. Paul alone. I will leave it to theologians to determine the right interpretation of his expressions; it appears to me that he only intended the abuse of nature, on man's part, and the great improvement in our nature which must follow from the improvement of the human race. . . . The whole world was always finite; and no one ever believed that it first became so by man's sin; but all finite existence is by its nature imperfect. Every finite object is limited and transitory, and when viewed separate from its connexion with the whole of which it is a part, we have sufficient cause to lament over the imperfection of the finite; but if we do not only regard the individual objects merely apart from the whole, and—if I may so express it—as if it were their duty to be independent, we shall be led to another mode of contemplation. The more an object constitutes an exclusive whole, the more we see in it the revelation of eternity. In the totality of the finite we first see the revelation of its eternal origin, so far, of course, as it is possible to see it from our point of view.'—*The Soul in Nature*, p. 189 (Bohn). The pantheistic bias of these statements seems mournfully apparent.

Note I, p. 8.

'The carnivora, organized to enjoy a life of rapine at the expense of the vegetable-feeders, to restrain their undue increase, and abridge the pangs of the maimed and the sickly, were duly adjusted in numbers, size, and ferocity to the fell task assigned to them in the organic economy of the pre-Adamite world. Beside a British tiger of larger size, and with proportionally larger paws than that of Bengal, there existed a stronger Feline animal (*Machairodus*) of equal size, which, from the great length and sharpness of its sabre-shaped canines, was probably the most ferocious and destructive of its peculiarly carnivorous family.'—Owen, *Hist. of British Fossil Mammals*, p. xxiv. Compare also Mantell, *Wonders of Geology*, Vol. i. p. 182 (Bohn).

Note J, p. 14.

It is slightly doubtful whether ὅτι is to be translated, as in the Vulgate, Claromontane, and our own Authorized Version, '*because*,' or—'*that*,' as apparently in the Syriac version, and as adopted by Fritzsche, De Wette, Meyer, and most recent commentators. The immediate connexion with ἐλπίδι in the latter sense seems so natural and direct (comp. Phil. i. 20), and the only counter-argument, —that the nominative αὐτὴ ἡ κτίσις would thus scarcely be repeated, is of so very little weight (for is there not a special and studied emphasis in the repetition?), that we may perhaps with confidence adopt the proposed translation. So apparently, Chrysostom, εἶπε δὴ, καὶ ποίᾳ ἐλπίδι; ὅτι καὶ αὐτὴ ἡ κτίσις ἐλευθερωθήσεται. Whether we connect ἐπ' ἐλπίδι with the finite verb ὑπετάγη (De Wette, Meyer), or with the participle ὑποτάξαντα (Chrys.), is perhaps of less consequence: the former construction, however, is to be preferred, as bringing ἐπ' ἐλπίδι into more distinct prominence, and as supplying an additional confirmation of the ἀποκαραδοκία of the creature.

Note K, p. 16.

Some interesting remarks on this subject will be found in Professor Schouw's work, *The Earth, Plants, and Man*, p. 228 sq. (Bohn), in which the action of man on nature, and the destruction that follows in the train of civilization, are calmly and fairly considered. On the whole, the opinion arrived at by Professor Schouw, though, perhaps, somewhat over-stated, seems approximately just, 'that in every case civilization richly recompenses the calamities that follow from it' (p. 239); still, considering the subject theologically, the fact of these *calamities* and often reckless destructions of vegetable life remains, and we have to consider how far the permissive כִּבְשֻׁהָ (Gen. i. 28) can in all cases be pleaded in justification. At any rate, and that is all with which we are now concerned, the violence done to nature is an acknowledged fact. With regard to the sort of *natural retribution* which follows on the reckless destruction of forests, the following remarks of Humboldt deserve consideration:—'When forests are destroyed, as they are everywhere in America by the European planters, with imprudent precipitancy, the springs are entirely dried up, or become less abundant. The beds of the rivers, remaining dry during a part of the year, are converted into torrents whenever great rains fall on the heights. As the sward and moss disappear with the brushwood from the sides of the mountains, the waters falling in rain are no longer impeded in their course; and instead of slowly augmenting the level of rivers by progressive filtrations, they furrow, during heavy showers, the sides of the hills, bearing down the loosened soil, and forming sudden and destructive inundations. Hence it results that the clearing of forests, the want of permanent springs, and the existence of torrents, are three phenomena closely connected together.'—Humboldt, *Travels in America*, Vol. ii. p. 9 (Bohn).

SERMON II.

NOTE A, p. 28.

Some curious thoughts on the creation of destructive animals will be found in an essay by Von Meyer, *Blätter für Höhere Wahrheit*, Vol. i. p. 342; comp. also Schlegel, *Philos. of Life*, p. 120 sq. (Bohn), who, however, has only superficially touched the subject, and on premises apparently not scientifically tenable. The statement of Kirby, *Bridgewater Treatise*, Vol. i. p. 61 (Bohn),—'that they [predaceous animals] must originally have eaten grass or straw, like the ox, and neither injured nor destroyed their fellow-beasts of a more harmless character,' —cannot be maintained in the face of modern geological discoveries. All, perhaps, on which we can safely insist is the really wide difference between a personal and progressive being like man and the non-personal and circumscribed individual of a genus; see Müller, *Lehre von d. Sünde*, Vol. ii. p. 389. Pain and suffering to us, and pain and suffering to them, seem, even at a first glance, to involve so many elements of difference, that we may as well take into consideration our own real ignorance, before we venture to question the fatherly beneficence of God. Arguments derived from the existence of various appliances on the part of the predatory animals, to shorten pain (Livingstone, *Travels*, p. 12), deserve consideration, but really make but a slight contribution towards even a partial solution of this profound and difficult question.

Note B, p. 29.

Though the early writers are not agreed as to the exact time when angels were created (see Augustine, *de Civ. Dei*, xi. 9), still the opinion that they existed before the world was created is very general (Ambrose, *Hexam.* I. 5. 19); nor are we without some traces of a supposed connexion between their fall, and, if not the creation, yet the final glorification of Man. Thus Augustine (*Enchirid.*, xxxix., comp. *de Civ. Dei*, xxii. 1) speaks of the 'partem hominum reparatam' as designed to supply the place of the lapsed angels. The exact opinion, however, here alluded to, is chiefly maintained in the works of the mystics of the seventeenth century; partially by Corn. Agrippa, *de Occult. Philos.*, but very distinctly by Behmen, who appears to have considered the creation of the world a sort of sequel on the fall of Lucifer: 'Auff dieses ist nun König Lucifer aus seinem königlichen Loco oder stuhl gestossen worden, welchen er an dem orthe hatte, wo erst der erschaffene Himmel ist, und ist allda bald die Schöpfung dieser Welt drauff gefolget,' *Aurora*, ch. ix. 44, comp. xviii. 10 sq. (Amst. 1682). Something similar appears to have been in the mind of Schlegel, when, in his fifth Lecture on the *Philosophy of Life*, he writes as follows :—' As then, by the death of the first man, who was not created for, nor originally designed for death, death has passed upon the whole human race ; so by the earlier fall of him, who had been the first and most glorious of created spirits, death passed upon the universe, that eternal death whose fire is unquenchable,' p. 90 (*Bohn*).

Note C, p. 30.

This statement must rely for its proof on the arguments of the first Sermon. It is satisfactory to observe that substantially the same view is maintained by one of the more able of the recent commentators on the Book of Genesis, Fr. Delitzsch, and by the able historian of the Old Testament, I. H. Kurtz. The words of this latter writer, as cited by Delitzsch, are remarkable, and worthy of citation :—' Die Natur bietet uns nicht mehr die reine Handschrift Gottes, sie ist in manchen Partien ein Palimpsest, ein *Codex rescriptus;* eine Feindeshand ist darüber gerathen.'—Delitzsch, *Genesis Ausgel.* p. 135. The question is discussed by Pye Smith (*Scripture and Science*, Lect. vii. 2), but apparently much embarrassed by regarding Vanity and Death as substantially identical. From the admirers of the ' Positive Philosophy,' as it is termed, I can expect but little sympathy ; I observe with sorrow, though not with surprise, that even the ' dogma of the condemnation of *mankind* through Adam,' is denounced by Comte, as ' morally more revolting than the dogma of exclusive salvation.' *Positive Philosophy*, Part vi. 9, Vol. ii. p. 276. (Translation by Martineau).

Note D, p. 33.

Some interesting remarks on the subject of Sheol will be found in Delitzsch, *System der Bibl. Psychol.* vi. 3, p. 353 sq., and in Hofmann, *der Schriftbeweis*, Vol. i. p. 499 sq. Several separate treatises on the state after death, as revealed in the Old Testament, have recently appeared in Germany. Of these may be specified Oehler, *Vet. Test. Sententia, &c.* (1846), and Bötticher, *de Inferis rebusque post mortem futuris, &c.* Dresden, 1846. To state, with great brevity, the distinction between the שְׁאוֹל of the Old, and ᾅδης of the New Testament, we may perhaps say,—that the latter does not seem to have been regarded as other than universal and all-embracing; whereas ᾅδης appears to us, in the New Testament (to borrow an epithet that has been applied to it), as 'bi-locular,' and as comprising *two* places of waiting—the one, παράδεισος for the souls of the holy, the other, ᾅδης proper, for the souls of the wicked.

Note E, p. 35.

See Gesenius, *Lexicon*, s. v. עַיִן p. DCXLIII. ed. Tregelles (London, 1847).

Note F, p. 33.

There seems clearly a close philological affinity between ΗΑΟ- and ΗΕΝΟ-. The principle on which this affinity depends has been termed the 'Evanescence of the nasal Liquid,' and has been well discussed by the late Dr. Donaldson, in a paper read before the Philological Society; *Transactions*, 1854, No. 14; see esp. p. 289.

Note G, p. 41.

For a fuller investigation of this difficult passage, see

Commentary on Phil. and Col. p. 139 (ed. 2), where the present view is investigated and explained at some length. The above interpretation has the authority of Augustine; and is maintained with only slight differences in detail, by Luther, Melancthon, Calvin, and Beza. The Romanist Church, on the contrary, as we might have anticipated, strongly presses the text as supporting the doctrine of the merits of the Saints, and their accumulated store of good works.

NOTE H. p. 48.

Though this seems to be a principle of the Divine government which, probably, few graver thinkers have not observed and verified, I do not remember to have seen it brought forward with such distinctness as it seems to deserve. It is noticed by Charnock in the following observations, which, though not by any means critically exact, will still bear citation :—' God proportions punishment to sin, and writes the cause of the judgment in the forehead of the judgment itself. Sodom burned in lust, and was consumed by fire from heaven. The Jews sold Christ for thirty pence, and, at the taking of Jerusalem, thirty of them were sold for a penny. So Adonibezek cut off the thumbs and great toes of others, and he is served in the same kind (Judges i. 7). The Babel-builders designed an indissoluble union, and God brings upon them unintelligible confusion. And in Exodus ix. 9, the ashes of the furnace, where the Israelites burnt the Egyptian bricks, sprinkled towards heaven, brought boils upon the Egyptians' bodies, that they might feel in their own what pain they had caused in the Israelites' flesh; and find, by the smart of the inflamed scab, what they had made the Israelites endure. The waters of the river Nile are turned into blood, wherein they had stifled the breath of the Israelites' infants; and at last the prince, and the flower of their nobility, are drowned in the Red Sea.'—*The Wisdom of God*, Part v. Vol. ii. p. 226 (ed. Parsons). Lond. 1815.

SERMON III.

Note A, p. 51.

The Scriptural aspects of the subject of death have been very ably noticed by Julius Müller, in his *Lehre von der Sünde*, Vol. ii. p. 388 sq.; to which excellent work I am indebted for several thoughts and suggestions that appear in this sermon. Of the more recent treatises on the subject, I may specify Krabbe, *Lehre von der Sünde und vom Tode*, Hamburg, 1836; Mau, *vom Tode dem Solde der Sünden*, Kiel, 1841; an article by Weisse on Eschatology, in the *Studien u. Kritiken*, for 1836, Part ii. p. 271 sq.; and a good sermon preached by the late Dean Buckland before the University of Oxford (Murray, 1839). For the more strictly psychological phenomena of death, see Schubert, *Geschichte der Seele*, Vol. ii. p. 434 sq.: and the treatise of Delitzsch, *Bibl. Psychologie*, vi. 1, p. 345 sq.; and finally, for the more purely scientific aspects of the subject of life generally, Whewell, *Philos. of Inductive Sciences*, Book ix., more esp. chap. ii. § 5.

Note B, p. 53.

See the comments of Weisse in *Studien v. Krit.* 1836, p. 282—294, esp. 292 sq., by whom this and similar views are briefly discussed.

Note C, p. 54.

The opinions here summed up in a single paragraph

will be found masqued in various disguises in the writings of most of those who belong to what is called the 'Progressive School' of thinkers. Sometimes these opinions will be found in combination with those noticed on page 53, sometimes alone. I make a single illustrative quotation from a sermon of Dr. Greenwood's, published in the 'Catholic Series' (Chapman, London), in which death is emphatically specified as an *appointment* :—'Our faculties themselves have their limits, beyond which there is no increase for them ; just as the body, when arrived at its full strength, grows no stronger. Here are indications of sufficient distinctness to show that there is only so much to be done in this life, so much to be known, so much to be experienced, and no more. And yet, together with these indications, there is an irrepressible desire in the bosom of man, who is thus limited and hemmed in, for the further expansion and progress which the terms of his present being deny to him. Death is appointed to fulfil this desire by removing the limits and restrictions which the initiatory state of existence imposes.'—Greenwood, *Sermons of Consolation*, p. 57, 58. If the reader has any interest in tracing out the lamentable hallucinations of modern thought, he will find the summary of clairvoyant opinions on natural death on page 413 of a large work, entitled the *Principles of Nature*, by Andrew Davis, 'the Poughkeepsie Seer,'—a work which it is unnecessary to characterize, but which, I sincerely regret to observe, has found an English publisher.

Note D, p 55.

See Müller, *Lehre von der Sünde*, Vol. ii. p. 391 ; and compare the argument between Augustine and Julian, *contra Jul.* iii. 156 sq. Vol. x. p. 1312 (Migne).

Note E, p. 56.

It is with great regret that I observe that even a writer so favourably known to the world as Dr. Lücke, the able editor of the Gospel, Epistles, and Revelation of St. John, should have lent the weight of his name to this most questionable, and I must add, most dangerous mode of interpretation; see the quotation in Usteri, *Paulin. Lehrb.* p. 362.

Note F, p. 59.

'When they were brought into existence, the word was—'*Let the waters bring forth—Let the earth bring forth,*' from which it would seem that God did not act *immediately* in their creation, except by His agency on those powers that He had established as rulers in nature, and by which He ordinarily taketh hold, as it were, of the material universe.'—Kirby, *Bridgewater Treatise*, Vol. i. p. 59. 60 (Bohn). The same appears to have been the opinion of Ambrose: 'Terra quoque semina resolvens, universa vivificat; et maxime tunc primum verbo Dei jussa viridescere, vivificationis suæ munere pullulabat,' *Hexameron*, Book v. 1; so, also, Augustine, *Confess.* xiii. 12, Basil, *Hexam.* viii. init.: comp. Bacon, *Advancement of Learning*, iv. 3, p. 172 (Bohn). For a brief notice of the Rabbinical opinions on this subject, see *Commentary on Genesis*, by Dr. Raphall, p. 4, and compare the remarks of Delitzsch, *Genesis Ausgelegt*, p. 74.

Note G, p. 59.

The likeness of man to his Maker is treated, though not very satisfactorily, by Ambrose, *Hexameron*, vi. 7. 8. How admirable are the words of Augustine: 'Sicut enim in nummo imago imperatoris aliter est, aliter in filio:

nam imago et imago est; sed aliter impressa est in nummo, aliter in filio, aliter in solido aureo imago imperatoris: sic et tu nummus Dei es, ex hoc melior, quia cum intellectu et cum quâdam vitâ nummus Dei es, ut scias etiam cujus imaginem geras, et ad cujus imaginem factus sis.'—*Serm.* ix. 8, Vol. v. p. 82 (ed. Migne).

Note H, p. 60.

See the admirable treatise *On the State of Man before the Fall*, Vol. ii. p. 70 (ed. Burton).

Note I, p. 60.

Μετέθηκε δὲ αὐτὸν ['Αδὰμ] ὁ Θεὸς ἐκ τῆς γῆς, ἐξ ἧς ἐγεγόνει, εἰς τὸν παράδεισον, διδοὺς αὐτῷ ἀφορμὴν προκοπῆς, ὅπως, αὐξάνων καὶ τέλειος γενόμενος, ἔτι δὲ καὶ Θεὸς ἀναδειχθείς, οὕτως καὶ εἰς τὸν οὐρανὸν ἀναβῇ, Theoph. *ad Autolyc.* cap. 24. This opinion, which seems to have been the traditional belief of the early Church, and which is nowhere better stated and expanded than in the 13th Book of Augustine *de Civitate Dei* (Vol. vii. p. 377–404, ed. Migne), is maintained by most of the more sober modern writers; comp. Buckland, *Sermon on Death*, p. 24; Holden, *on the Fall of Man*, p. 240 (Lond. 1823); Pye Smith, *Scripture and Geology*, Lect. VII. 2, p. 263 (Bohn).

Note J, p. 61.

The following words of Augustine are particularly clear and pertinent: 'Aliud est non posse mori, sicut quasdam naturas immortales creavit Deus; aliud est autem posse non mori, secundum quem modum primus creatus est homo immortalis; quod ei præstabatur de ligno vitæ, non de constitutione naturæ; a quo ligno separatus est cum peccasset, ut posset mori; qui nisi peccasset, posset non mori.'—*de Genesi ad Literam,* vi. 25, Vol. iii. p. 354 (ed. Migne); see also *de Civit. Dei,* xiii. 20.

Note K, p. 62.

See Müller, *Lehre von der Sünde,* Vol. ii. p. 394: compare also Buckland, *Serm. on Death,* p. 21, who, however, does not seem to seize the point, that the execution of the sentence actually commenced at the very hour of the declaration of it, in the pains and sufferings which all tended to, and accelerated its final completion and consummation: compare Augustine *de Civit. Dei,* xiii. 23.

Note L, p. 63.

See Gesenius, *Lexicon,* s. v. שׁוּב, who supports his opinion by an appeal to ancient versions and commentaries. The point does not seem to have been much noticed in modern commentaries: Tuch passes it over *in loc.,* but briefly denies it on p. 121. Knobel silently reproduces the usual translation. The version of the LXX is distinct enough, ἐν ἱδρῶτι τοῦ προσώπου σου φαγῇ τὸν ἄρτον σου, ἕως τοῦ ἀποστρέψαι σε εἰς τὴν γῆν ἐξ ἧς ἐλήφθης.

Note M, p. 64.

See Mau, *vom Tode,* p. 101, who appears to rest his affirmation on the supposed universality of the declaration in 1 Cor. xv. 22. Let us rather hear Augustine: 'Non erat Illi unde haberet mortem; non habebamus nos unde haberemus vitam: accepit Ille mortem de nostro, ut daret nobis vitam de suo.' *Serm.* CCXXXII. 5, Vol. v. p. 1110 (ed. Migne).

Note N, p. 66.

The objects of the Transfiguration were perhaps threefold: First, it might have been mercifully designed to convince the disciples of their Master's divinity, and to prepare them for bearing up against the sad scenes of His passion which so soon followed. Secondly, it appears to have had what may be termed a 'dispensational' aspect; *i.e.* it was in accordance with the eternal counsels of God, that there was to be a formal, and as it were, visible incorporation of the Law and the Prophets in the Gospel. Thirdly, there may have been involved in it some deeper mysteries, similar, or analogous to what is here alluded to. That it was an act of divine intercourse to prepare our Lord for His sufferings, as maintained by Bp. Thompson (Sermon, 1850), appears somewhat doubtful.

Note O, p. 67.

A clear discussion of the three opinions commonly maintained on this very deep and mysterious subject will be found in an article by Dr. Edward Robinson in the *Bibliotheca Sacra* for 1835, p. 292—312. See also *Lectures on the Life of our Lord*, p. 369, note, p. 395, note.

SERMON IV.

Note A, p. 78.

Several good articles on modern poetry, and specifications of some of its objectionable theories in respect to the doctrines of the Last Things, will be found in the *Christian Remembrancer*: see especially Vol. xxi. p. 389 sq., Vol. xxiv. p. 319 sq. Of the general tendencies, in this respect, of some of the most popular of our modern novels, it is scarcely necessary to add proofs. I may, however, here mention, and venture to express my regret, that the author of so manly and Christian a work as *Tom Brown's School-days*, should have so far yielded to the current of popular persuasions as to have sketched out, in the dream that Arthur relates (p. 353), a final adjustment which, to say the least, is not theologically demonstrable.

Note B, p. 79.

It is unnecessary to say that I am here alluding to the concluding essay appended to Mr. Maurice's *Theological Essays*, and published separately (Cambr. 1854). It is easy to understand how a writer, whose heart is so truly wide, and whose sympathies are so noble and generous, should have been led into unguarded statements upon this momentous subject. Such statements are, however, not the less to be deplored. In a feeling sermon on *Death and Life*, preached in Lincoln's Inn Chapel, in March, 1855. I much regret to observe the following words : ' I know well that when we see a fellow-creature plunging down deeper and deeper into the abyss,—when we think he has taken the final plunge, and when then, just then, the voice is heard saying to him, ' Thy soul shall be required of thee,' —and when in our dimness and horror of mind, there seems no reason why we should not have been—why we may not be —like him, it appears for a moment as if the case for him and for us had been made more terrible by Christ's death and resurrection, because they tell of a love slighted and *resisted*, which no other acts could tell us of. But when the waters have almost overwhelmed us, when we have come to the deep mire where no standing is, we discover, I believe, that *we are blaspheming God* by such thoughts ; that, after all, the faith that Christ died and rose again gives us a hope for ourselves and *for the universe*, which, without this, we must soon lose altogether ; that while we believe this, though we must be believing in the eternal union of sin and misery, we become absolutely unable to determine by our measures what victory may yet remain for love over sin ; whether the rebellious spirit may not have been stopped in a career where all persons and circumstances were probably abetting its ruin, on purpose that it might be subjected to *other* methods of cure,' p. 15. Though there is a depth of feeling in all this which no one ought lightly to esteem, —yet can it be doubted that these statements involve *serious* error? If I rightly understand a sentence somewhat long and embarrassed, the summary seems to be,— that a resister of Christ here on earth may be removed for final cure to another sphere. But for this have we any authority in Scripture whatever? Does not this seriously militate against the declaration of an Apostle,—κατὰ δὲ τὴν σκληρότητά σου καὶ ἀμετανόητον καρδίαν θησαυρίζεις σεαυτῷ ὀργὴν ἐν ἡμέρᾳ ὀργῆς καὶ ἀποκαλύψεως δικαιοκρισίας τοῦ Θεοῦ, ὃς ἀποδώσει ἑκάστῳ κατὰ τὰ ἔργα αὐτοῦ, Rom. ii. 5, 6,—words *very* definite?

Note C, p. 79.

Most of the modern views of a universal restitution of good and bad alike, and most of their assaults on the doctrine of the eternity of future punishments, will be found to turn on mistaken views of the true idea and meaning of punishment. See some good remarks in Müller, *Lehre von der Sünde,* Vol. ii. p. 559 sq., and a long, difficult, but in many points satisfactory article on Eternal Condemnation, by Erbkam, in the *Studien u. Kritiken,* for 1838; see esp. p. 422 sq.

Note D, p. 80.

'Qui (Deus) de mortali progenie merito justeque damnatâ tantum populum gratiâ suâ colligit, ut inde suppleat, et instauret partem quae lapsa est angelorum; ac sic illa dilecta et superna civitas non fraudetur suorum numero civium, quin etiam fortassis et uberiore laetetur.'

—Augustine, *de Civitate Dei*, Book xxii. 1 ; compare ib. *Enchirid.* ch. xxix. Vol. vii. p. 246 (ed. Migne).

Note E, p. 81.

This oneness of the race as evinced in the creation, appears to have been felt, if not distinctly expressed by some of the early writers ; '*Et fecit Deus hominem, ad imaginem Dei fecit eum* (Gen. i. 27); ut sicut Deus unus est, unus ab eo fieret homo : ut quomodo ex Deo uno omnia, ita ex uno homine omne genus esset super faciem totius terræ. Unus igitur unum fecit, qui unitatis ejus haberet imaginem.'—*Comment. on Col.* iii. 8 sq., doubtfully ascribed to Ambrose (Vol. iv. p. 436, ed. Migne).

Note F, p. 81.

On this command see the excellent remarks of Bishop Bull, *State of Man before the Fall*, Vol. ii. p. 66 (ed. Burton), and compare Holden, *On the Fall*, Sect. viii. p. 210 sq.

Note G, p. 82.

See the remarks of Hengstenberg, *Christology*, Vol. i. p. 18 (Clark), who appears in this respect to have modified his former opinions. The only fault in his present interpretation is this ; that he appears to have too much given up the reference of the prophecy to the Messiah. Even if we do not say that it refers to the Messiah specifically and exclusively, we can scarcely overlook the distinct implicit reference. At any rate we shall not be much moved by the flat denial of Priaulx, *Quæstiones Mosaicæ*, p. 98 (ed. 2, 1854). Further remarks on this passage will be found in Hofmann, *Schriftb.* Vol. i. p. 194 sq.

Note H, p. 83.

'Da das Weib der Schlange gegenüber den über das

Loos der Menscheit entscheidenden Schritt gethan hat, so ist sie hier Repräsentantin des ganzen Geschlechts: Gott setzt zwischen der Schlange und dem Weibe, aber nicht blos zwischen den gegenwärtigen Individuen, sondern zugleich zwischen den *Schlangensamen* und *Weibessamen*, d. h. zwischen dem gesammten Schlangen und Menschengeschlecht einen unversöhnlichen Hass, einen Krieg ohne Frieden.'—Delitzsch, *Genesis Ausgelegt*, p. 130.

NOTE I, p. 83.

For the detail of this interpretation, see the commentary of Meyer *in loc.* The following objections of Dean Alford to the usual interpretation seem correct and pertinent: '$ἦν$ cannot as in Erasm., Luther, Calv., Beza, al., and E. V., belong to $ἐν\ Χριστῷ$, ' God *was in Christ*, reconciling,' &c.,—partly on account of the position of $ἐν\ Χρ.$, which would thus probably be before $ἦν$, but principally (Meyer) because of the incoherence with $θέμενος\ ἐν\ ἡμῖν\ κ.\ τ.\ λ.$: for in that case the two latter clauses must express the *manner* of reconciliation by Christ, which the second of them does not.' *Comment. in loc.* Perhaps we may say that the Apostle was proceeding regularly with $ἦν\ καταλλάσσων$, when the thought of Him, in whom, and in whom alone the $καταλλαγή$ was realized and had its effects, caused him to introduce the vital words $ἐν\ Χριστῷ$, ' God was—in Christ—reconciling,' &c.

NOTE J, p. 87.

The remark of Augustine, which seems to limit the application of this text, will be found in his *Tractat. in Joann.* cx. 4, Vol. iii. p. 1923 (ed. Migne), where, having previously investigated the declaration ' ut omnes unum sint' (John xvii. 21), and defined the ' omnes' to be the ' mundus credens,' he proceeds : ' Ipsi sunt enim mundus,

non permanens inimicus, qualis est mundus damnationi
prædestinatus; sed ex inimico amicus effectus, propter
quem 'Deus erat in Christo mundum reconcilians sibi.''
His remarks that follow on the exact *nature* of the reconciliation
are worthy of citation; 'Quod ergo reconciliati
sumus Deo per mortem Filii ejus, non sic audiatur, non
sic accipiatur, quasi ideo nos reconciliaverit ei Filius, ut
jam inciperet amare quos oderat; sicut reconciliatur inimicus
inimico, ut deinde sint amici, et invicem diligant
qui oderant invicem; sed *jam nos diligenti* reconciliati
sumus ei, cum quo propter peccatum inimicitias habebamus,'
ib. § 6. If I rightly understand the 'jam nos
diligenti,' as distinguished from the preceding 'jam inciperet
amare,' the sentiment is approximately the same
with that expressed in the sermon. Augustine's only incorrectness
(if *I* may presume to use such an expression)
is in his obvious desire throughout the Tractate to narrow
the meaning of 'mundus.' Compare Bp. Thompson,
Bampton Lectures, Lect. vii. p. 192, who however in his
note *in loc.* is scarcely accurate in assuming that in Rom.
v. 19, οἱ πολλοί = πάντες.

Note K, p. 87.

On the belief in the progressiveness of mankind, see
some excellent remarks in Hare, *Guesses at Truth*, Series
ii. p. 27 sq. I make the following extract from the concluding
portion of the essay: 'The progress of mankind
is not in a straight line uniform and unbroken. On the
contrary, it is subject to manifold vicissitudes, interruptions,
and delays; *ever advancing on the whole* indeed, but
often receding in one quarter, while it pushes forward in
another; and sometimes even retreating altogether for a
while that it may start afresh with greater and more irresistible
force,' p. 62.

Note L, p. 89.

For a discussion of this very difficult text, and for a justification of the translation adopted in the text of the Sermon, I must take the liberty of referring to my Commentary on *Coloss. l. c.*, p. 131 sq. (ed. 2). The view there adopted, according to which τῆς θεότητος is to be regarded as the supplement to τὸ πᾶν πλήρωμα, and the whole regarded, as an abstract and sublime designation of the Deity, seems to commend itself from its simplicity. At any rate, whatever construction is adopted, the main declarations of this solemn text remain the same.

Note M, p. 92.

Here again I must refer to my Commentary for details. My friend, Dean Alford, appears to dissent from my interpretation of the preposition ἀνά, in the compound ἀνακεφαλαιώσασθαι. Up to the present time, I have seen no reason to modify my views: ἀνά, both here and Rom. xiii. 9 (see Meyer), appears to imply more than mere summation *upward* of a list of items. Would not κεφαλαιόω, a word defined by Hesychius as equivalent to συντόμως συνάγειν, and not of uncommon occurrence (Thucyd. iii. 67, vi. 91), have otherwise been quite sufficient? Ἀνακεφαλαίωσις is defined by Quintilian, *de Inst. Orator.* vi. 7, as 'rerum *repetitio* et congregatio.'

Note N, p. 89.

See especially Bishop Pearson, *Creed*, Art. vi., who speaks of Christ's everlasting Kingly power in the following accurate and exalted language: 'The dominion which He hath was given Him as a reward for what He suffered: and certainly the reward shall not cease when the work is done: He hath promised to make us kings and priests, which honour we expect in heaven, believing we shall *reign with* Him for ever, and therefore for ever must believe Him King. *The kingdoms of this world are become the kingdoms of the Lord, and of His Christ, and He shall reign for ever and ever,* not only to the modificated eternity of His mediatorship, so long as there shall be need of regal power to subdue the enemies of God's elect; but also to the complete eternity of the duration of His humanity, which for the future is co-eternal to His divinity,' p. 283 (ed. 1701).

Note O, p. 95.

The remark, attributed to Clement of Alexandria, Βία ἐχθρὸν Θεῷ is one that should never be forgotten in our attempts to reason on the counsels and providences of God. Compare *Epist. ad Diogn.* cap. 7, Βία οὐ πρόσεστι τῷ Θεῷ.

Note P, p. 96.

Some of the opinions here alluded to are commonly connected with the name of Origen, and apparently with justice: see esp. *de Principiis*, Book I. ch. 6, where he fully discusses the subject of the Consummation of all things. In sec. 6, he speaks definitely of the possible restitution of evil men and angels,—' ut alii in primis, alii in secundis, nonnulli etiam in ultimis temporibus, et per majora ac graviora supplicia, nec non et diuturna ac multis, ut ita dicam, saeculis tolerata, asperioribus emendationibus reparati, et restituti eruditionibus primo angelicis tum deinde etiam superiorum graduum virtutibus, et sic per singula ad superiora provecti usque ad ea quae sunt invisibilia et aeterna, perveniant,' Vol. xxi. p. 111 (ed. Lomm.). See a summary of these views in Jerome. *Epist.* xciv. (ad Avitum). It should be remembered, however, that this great and able writer not only acknowledged that such teaching was dangerous for the unconverted (*contra Celsum*, vi. 27), but in some of his works uses very definite language in favour of a popular reception of the Catholic doctrine; see for example the somewhat curious fluctuation of opinion pervading *Hom. xix. in Jerem.* The real basis of Origen's opinions seems to have been a general persuasion that what was incomplete in this world would be adjusted and completed in the next; and with that belief modern thought has much in common. On the somewhat liberal opinions of some even of the orthodox Fathers, see Hagenbach, *Hist. of Doctrines*, § 142, Vol. i. p. 383 sq. (Clark).

Note Q, p. 101.

On this subject see the profound remarks of Müller, *Lehre von der Sünde*, Book v. His comments on the development of sin in our race as bound to the *law of gradation*, deserve great consideration; see esp. Vol. ii. p. 570 sq., where the persistence and progress in evil is sketched out with striking and tragic power.

SERMON V.

Note A, p. 103.

The passage referred to is in Book v. ch. 6, p. 300 (ed. Mass.), where the subject of man's constitution is treated at some length. The following extract may be made:—
'Neque enim plasmatio carnis ipsa secundum se homo perfectus est; sed corpus hominis, et pars hominis. Neque enim et anima ipsa secundum se homo; sed anima hominis, et pars hominis. Neque Spiritus homo. Spiritus enim, et non homo vocatur. Commixtio autem et unitio horum omnium, perfectum hominem efficit.' Then follows a

distinct reference to, and an explanation of our present text. The whole chapter in Irenæus should be read *in extenso*.

Note B, p. 106.

'Mortal body and immortal soul are [in our popular pulpit language] so pointedly and continually set in mutual contrast, and assigned to different lots, that all view of the future life of the former seems to be absorbed in the exclusive notion of the eternal state of the latter. How strange does such omission appear, when we turn round from such preaching, and hear our Lord warning us, that not only our body, but our soul also [Matth. x. 28], may be destroyed in hell.'—Evans, *Ministry of the Body*, p. 7.

Note C, p. 106.

By 'doubtful application' I mean that if we desire to use strict language, we must rather speak of the immortality of the 'spirit.' It is to the union of the latter with the former that most modern psychologists ascribe the true immortality of the soul; comp. Delitzsch, *Bibl. Psychol.* vi. 2, p. 350. An admirable article on the grounds on which some of the ante-Nicene Fathers spoke of the soul as *mortal*, will be found in Olshausen, *Opuscula*, p. 167 sq.; see esp. p. 174.

Note D, p. 107.

The epithet ὁλόκληρον occupies the position of a secondary predication, and would be technically termed by modern grammarians a 'secondary predicate:' see esp. Donaldson, *New Crat.* § 302, who has justly the credit of first bringing the subject of 'secondary' and 'tertiary' predicates clearly and distinctly before the English reader. Some further statements will be found in Müller, *Kleine Schriften*, Vol. i. p. 310; comp. notes *on Coloss.* ii. 3.

Note E, p. 107.

On the meaning of this word, and its distinction from τέλειος, see the good remarks of Trench, *Synonyms of the New Testament*, § xxii.

Note F, p. 109.

The remarks of De Wette on this text are rather suicidal. 'In τὸ πνεῦμα καὶ ἡ ψυχή ist die richtige psychologische Unterscheidung des Animalischen (an die sinnliche Erregung Geknüpften) und des Geistigen (Vernünftigen) in der innern Natur des Menschen, wie sie auch Hebr. iv. 12, bei Philo und Plato vorkommt nicht zu verkennen . . . Jedoch hat sie hier bloss *rhetorische* Bedeutung,' *Erklärung d. Briefe an die Thess.* p. 126.

Note G, p. 111.

On this very difficult text see the comments of Ebrard, Lünemann, and of the recent and able editor, Delitzsch.

Note H, p. 112.

See especially the excellent remarks of Ebrard on the first and superficial effect of the Gospel on the ψυχή, and then its deeper and more penetrating character when it enters into 'the watchfully conscious life of the thoughts,' and obtains a place for itself in the 'sphere of the conscious will and voluntary thought.' The passage is somewhat too long for citation, but well deserves perusal.

Note I, p. 112.

See Meyer *in loc.*, who has briefly, but clearly, explained the full meaning and force of this passage. How coarse and inexact is the language we meet with in some of the commentaries on this noble Epistle, which find reception with a certain class of thinkers: 'The natural Body is an organism fitted for the development and action of the *animal* man; the spiritual Body is an organism fitted for the development and action of the spiritual nature; and the spiritual Body holds to the natural Body a relation which is emblemed by that which the most glorious of Nature's forms bears to the seed from which it springs.' —Thom, *on the Corinthians*, p. 239 (London. 1851).

NOTE J, p. 113.

This is very clearly stated by Olshausen in his excellent article, 'De naturæ humanæ trichotomiâ N. T. scriptoribus receptâ,' (*Opuscula*, p. 157), an article to which I have been greatly indebted in the composition of this sermon. The only fault is that it is too short, and does not define with quite sufficient accuracy the lines of demarcation between the usages of πνεῦμα and νοῦς, and between ψυχή and some of the terms (p. 160), which stand in most common connexion with it. For these points the student is referred to Beck, *Seelenlehre* (a short, but good treatise), Delitzsch, *Bibl. Psychologie*, and the large general work of Schubert, *Geschichte der Seele*, Vol. ii. p. 498, sq.

NOTE K, p. 113.

For a very able discussion on the meaning of the term σάρξ, see Müller, *Lehre von der Sünde*, Vol. i. p. 444 sq. Some good remarks by Tholuck will be found in a recent article in the *Studien u. Kritiken*, for 1855, in which the views of Müller, who perhaps too rigorously excludes *all* ideas of sensationalism, are mainly substantiated, but, in some cases, apparently beneficially expanded. See also notes *on Coloss.* ii. 11.

Note L, p. 115.

See Job vii. 15, ἀπαλλάσσεις δὲ ἀπὸ πνεύματος τὴν ψυχήν μου, ἀπὸ δὲ θανάτου τὰ ὀστᾶ μου; where the Hebrew is וַתִּבְחַר מַחֲנָק נַפְשִׁי מָוֶת מֵעַצְמוֹתָי. On the punctuation and meaning of this somewhat difficult verse, see Hirzel in the *Handbuch zum Alten Test.*, Part ii. p. 48.

Note M, p. 115.

In Philo a similar distinction is maintained, but under somewhat different terms and divisions. The following passage may be adduced as one of the most distinct: τρία γὰρ μέρη ψυχῆς, τὸ μὲν θρεπτικόν, τὸ δὲ αἰσθητικόν, τὸ δὲ λογικόν. τοῦ μὲν οὖν λογικοῦ τὸ θεῖον πνεῦμα οὐσία, κατὰ τὸ θεολόγον. φησὶ γάρ, ὅτι ἐνεφύσησεν εἰς τὸ πρόσωπον αὐτοῦ πνοὴν ζωῆς. τοῦ δὲ αἰσθητικοῦ καὶ ζωτικοῦ τὸ αἷμα οὐσία. Λέγει γὰρ ἐν ἑτέροις, ὅτι ψυχὴ πάσης σαρκὸς αἷμά ἐστιν· καὶ κυριώτατα ψυχὴν σαρκὸς αἷμα εἴρηκε, *Fragmenta*, Vol. ii. p. 668 (ed. Mang.); see also *Leg. Alleg.* i. Vol. i. p. 57 (ed. Mang). According to Philo we should perhaps have to number four principles, the body, and the three principles above enumerated; see Bull, *State of Man, &c.* Vol. ii. p. 91 sq. (ed. Burton).

Note N, p. 115.

The words of the original are, Ἔπλασεν ὁ Θεὸς τὸν ἄνθρωπον χοῦν ἀπὸ τῆς γῆς λαβών, καὶ πνεῦμα ἐνῆκεν αὐτῷ καὶ ψυχήν, *Archæol.* i. 1. 2.

Note O, p. 115.

A large collection of passages from Rabbinical writers will be found in that laborious work, which we owe to the liberality of a former King of Prussia, the *Entdecktes Judenthum* of Eisenmenger, Vol. i. p. 887 sq. On the nature of the Neshama (נְשָׁמָה), and the meaning assigned to it by the earlier and later Rabbinical writers, see Bishop Bull, *State of Man before the Fall*, Vol. ii. p. 93 (ed. Burton).

Note P, p. 115.

A pertinent quotation from Irenæus will be found in Note A, but the whole chapter (Book v. ch. 6) should be carefully read as being peculiarly clear and explicit. The following is the passage alluded to from Justin Martyr; ψυχὴ ἐν σώματί ἐστιν, οὐ ζῇ δὲ ἄψυχον. Σῶμα ψυχῆς ἀπολειπούσης οὐκ ἔστιν. Οἶκος γὰρ τὸ σῶμα ψυχῆς· πνεύματος δὲ ψυχὴ οἶκος, *Fragmenta*, p. 1589 (ed. Migne). Out of many passages from Clement of Alexandria we may quote as follows : ἐκ γῆς μὲν τὸ σῶμα διαπλάττεσθαι λέγει ὁ Μωϋσῆς, ὃ γήινόν φησιν ὁ Πλάτων σκῆνος. Ψυχὴν δὲ τὴν λογικὴν ἄνωθεν ἐμπνευσθῆναι ὑπὸ τοῦ Θεοῦ εἰς πρόσωπον. ἐνταῦθα γὰρ τὸ ἡγεμονικὸν ἱδρύσθαι λέγουσι τὴν διὰ τῶν αἰσθητηρίων ἐπεισόδιον τῆς ψυχῆς ἐπὶ τοῦ πρωτοπλάστου εἴσοδον ἑρμηνεύοντες, *Strom*. vi. 14. 94.

Origen writes as follows : 'Frequenter in Scripturis invenimus, et a nobis sæpe dissertum est, quod homo spiritus, et corpus, et anima esse dicatur. Verum cum dicitur quia 'caro concupiscit adversus spiritum, spiritus autem adversus carnem,' media proculdubio ponitur anima, quæ vel desideriis spiritus acquiescat, vel ad carnis concupiscentias inclinetur,' *Comment. in Rom.* i. 18, Vol. vi. p. 56 (ed. Lomm.). The passage further alluded to as quoted by Hammond, and of which the thoughts on p. 117 are a reminiscence, is longer, and will be found in his note on this text. The words of this great writer are perhaps still more explicit in his *Comment. in Joannem*, wherehe thus writes : καὶ ταῦτα ζητεῖν ἐτόλμησα μετρίως, τηρήσας ἐν πάσῃ τῇ γραφῇ διαφορὰν ψυχῆς καὶ πνεύματος, καὶ μέσον μέν τι θεωρῶν εἶναι τὴν ψυχήν, καὶ ἐπιδεχομένην ἀρετὴν καὶ κακίαν, ἀνεπίδεκτον δὲ τῶν χειρόνων τὸ πνεῦμα τοῦ ἀνθρώπου τὸ ἐν αὐτῷ· τὰ γὰρ κάλλιστα καρποὶ λέγονται εἶναι τοῦ πνεύματος, οὐχ ὡς ἂν οἰηθείη τις τοῦ ἁγίου, ἀλλὰ τοῦ ἀνθρώπου, xxxii. 11. vol. ii. p. 433 (ed. Lomm.). The last remark, however, that the human πνεῦμα is ἀνεπίδεκτον τῶν χειρόνων, may be decidedly questioned. To hazard a passing remark on a most profound subject, does not sin against the Holy Ghost involve some such awful condition as this,—that the human πνεῦμα so far loses, so to say, the very characteristics of its true nature, as to array itself in fearful antagonism against the Holy Spirit? Compare some thoughts of Müller, *Lehre von der Sünde*, Vol. ii. p. 592. Some remarks on the psychological views of Origen will be found in Neander, *Church History*, Vol. ii. p. 397 (Clark). The following are the words of Didymus on our text; 'Ad Thessalonicenses quoque: *integer* inquit, *spiritus vester, et anima, et corpus*. Sicut etiam alia est anima, et corpus aliud: sic et aliud est spiritus ab animâ quæ suo loco specialiter appellatur. De quo et oravit, ut integer cum animâ servetur et corpore, quia incredibile est et blasphemum, orare Apostolum, ut Spiritus sanctus integer servetur, qui nec imminutionem potest recipere nec profectum. De humano ergo, ut diximus, spiritu in hoc Apostoli sermo testatus est,' *de Spir. Sancto*, § 55, translated by Jerome, Vol. ii. p. 148 (ed. Migne). Gregory of Nyssa, after stating that man is composed of three parts, thus justifies his assertion; καθὼς καὶ παρὰ τοῦ ἀποστόλου τὸ τοιοῦτον ἐμάθομεν, ἐν οἷς πρὸς τοὺς Ἐφεσίους [Θεσσαλονικεῖς] ἔφη, προσευχόμενος αὐτοῖς τὴν ὁλοτελῆ χάριν τοῦ σώματος, καὶ τῆς ψυχῆς, καὶ τοῦ πνεύματος, ἐν τῇ παρουσίᾳ τοῦ Κυρίου φυλαχθῆναι, *de Hominis Opif.* vii. p. 60 (Paris, 1615). The remark of Basil will be found in *Epist.* ccxxxiii. (ed. Bened. 1839).

NOTE Q, p. 116.

The exact heresy of Apollinaris is so often incorrectly stated, as if it consisted in denying that our Lord had any human soul, that it may be as well to subjoin the following specific statement from Theodoret ; σαρκωθῆναι τὸν Θεὸν ἔφησε λόγον, σῶμα καὶ ψυχὴν ἀνειληφότα. οὐ τὴν λογικήν, ἀλλὰ τὴν ἄλογον, ἣν φυσικὴν ἤγουν ζωτικὴν τινες ὀνομάζουσι· τὸν δὲ νοῦν ἄλλο τι παρὰ τὴν ψυχὴν εἶναι λέγων, οὐκ ἔφησεν ἀνειλῆφθαι, ἀλλ᾽ ἀρκέσαι τὴν θείαν φύσιν εἰς τὸ πληρῶσαι τοῦ νοῦ τὴν χρείαν. *Hæret. Fab.* iv. 8. This very definite statement seems distinctly to justify the opinion advanced, p. 112. Apollinaris pressed the generally received doctrine of the trichotomy in our nature, that he might define more precisely his views of our Lord's spiritual nature and of the exact way in which it differed from our own. In a word, he acknowledged that our Lord had a σῶμα and ψυχή, but he denied His having a human πνεῦμα; this part according to his views being occupied by τὸ Πνεῦμα. Apollinaris was rightly condemned by the council of Constantinople, A.D. 381; but it may be well to remember that his error arose from a desire to do greater honour to the Eternal Son, not to detract from it, like Arius and his followers. On the heresy of Apollinaris, see Hagenbach, *Hist. of Doctrines*, § 99, Vol. i. p. 270 (Clark), and Bishop Pearson, *Creed*, Art. iii. p. 159 (ed. 1669); and on the doctrine of the trichotomy in reference to our Lord's nature, as maintained by some of the earlier writers, see Neander, *Church History*, Vol. ii. p. 401 sq. (Clark).

Note R, p. 116.

In his treatise *on the Soul* Tertullian very emphatically opposes the idea of any absolute division between the soul and spirit: 'Denique si separas spiritum et animam, separa et opera; agant in discreto aliquid ambo, seorsum anima, seorsum spiritus: anima sine spiritu vivat, spiritus sine animâ spiret; alterum relinquat corpora, alterum remaneat, mors et vita conveniant. Si enim duo sunt anima et spiritus, *dividi possunt*, ut divisione eorum, alterius discedentis, alterius immanentis mortis et vitæ concursus eveniat,' *de Animâ*, cap. x. Vol. ii. p. 663 (ed. Migne). The italicized words, however, and the general current of the treatise (see esp. cap. xiii.), show what Tertullian was particularly condemning. A distinction between the united parts he might, under limitations, have admitted; the idea of an actual separation and *division* he opposed and denied. The remarks of Augustine, alluded to in the text, will be found in his treatise *de Animâ*, iv. 32, Vol. x. p. 544 (ed. Migne).

Note S, p. 117.

The opinion of Hammond will be found in his Commentary on this passage; that of Bishop Bull, in his treatise above alluded to, *The State of Man before the Fall*, Vol. ii. p. 93 sq.; that of Jackson, in his admirable work on the *Creed*, Vol. ix. p. 236 (Oxf. 1844).

Note T, p. 118.

On the Neshama of the Rabbins, see above, note O. For the readers of Rabbinical Hebrew, I make the following extract from Buxtorf *Lex. Chald. et Rabb.*, s. v. p. 1403. 'de differentiâ נֶפֶשׁ *animæ*, רוּחַ 'spiritus,' et נְשָׁמָה vide Aben Esram, *Eccl.* vii. 5.'

Note U, p. 119.

The arguments of Bishop Bull will be found in his *State of Man, &c.*, Vol. ii. p. 96 sq., where he opposes Didymus, but, I venture to think, with but little success. Bull's theory is, in fact, really a 'tetrachotomy'—body, soul, spirit, and Holy Spirit. The words of Irenæus, which, *taken apart* from the context and current of the chapter, seem certainly in his favour, are as follows: 'Anima autem et Spiritus pars hominis esse possunt, homo autem nequaquam: perfectus autem homo commixtio et adunitio est animae assumentis Spiritum Patris, et admixta ei carni, quæ est plasmata secundum imaginem Dei,' *contr. Hær.* v. 6. As, however, has before been said, the whole chapter ought to be carefully perused to arrive exactly at the views of this ancient writer. Chrysostom *in loc.*, thus writes:—τὸ πνεῦμα τί φησιν ἐνταῦθα ; τὸ χάρισμα. ἂν μὲν γὰρ ἔχοντες λαμπάδας τὰς λαμπάδας ἀπέλθωμεν, εἰσελευσόμεθα εἰς τὸν νυμφῶνα· ἂν δὲ ἐσβεσμένας, οὐκέτι. Διὰ τοῦτό φησιν, Ὁλόκληρον ὑμῶν τὸ πνεῦμα· ἐκείνου γὰρ μένοντος ἀκεραίου, καὶ τοῦτο μένει.

SERMON VI.

Note A, p. 130.

The passage referred to is towards the close of the article on the Communion of Saints, where Bishop Pearson thus writes: 'This communion of saints in heaven and earth, upon the mystical union of Christ their Head, being fundamental and internal, what acts or external operations it produceth, is not so certain. That we communicate with them in hope of that happiness which they actually enjoy, is evident; that we have the Spirit of God given us as an earnest, and so a part of their felicity, is certain. But what they do in heaven in relation to us on earth, particularly considered, or what we ought to perform in reference to them in heaven, beside a reverential respect and study of imitation, is not revealed to us in the Scriptures, nor can be concluded by necessary deduction from any principles of Christianity.' p. 357 (ed. 1669).

Note B, p. 131.

For a verification of this statement, see Bingham, *Antiquities*, Book xv. chap. iii. § 15 ; and especially Usher, *Answer to a Jesuit*, Vol. iii. p. 201 sq. (ed. Elrington), where examples are given at length. See also Palmer, *Origines Liturgicæ*, chap. iv. 10, Vol. ii. p. 94 sq., and Bona, *Res Liturgicæ*, Book ii. xiv. p. 450.

Note C, p. 132.

The theory of a παννυχία of the soul, as it was termed, was rejected by all the more earnest thinkers of antiquity. On this theory see esp. Delitzsch, *Bibl. Psychol.* p. 360 sq., West, *Studien u. Kritiken*, for the current year, p. 278 sq., and also the elaborate note of Koch, *on* 1 *Thess.* iv. 13.

Note D, p. 134.

The words as translated from the Coptic in the large work of Renaudot are, ' Memento Domine patrum fratrumque nostrorum, qui obdormierunt, quieveruntque in fide orthodoxâ.' *Liturg. Orient.* p. 9. A longer and less restricted form for those 'qui dormierunt et quieverunt in Sacerdotio et *omni* ordine laicorum' will be found on p. 18. In the Liturgy of the Church of Constantinople the words are simply ἔτι προσφέρομέν σοι τὴν λογικὴν ταύτην λατρείαν ὑπὲρ τῶν ἐν πίστει ἀναπαυσαμένων προπατέρων, πατέρων, πατριφαχῶν, κ. τ. λ., Usher p. 202. For an account of this ancient liturgy, the text of which has been pronounced to be doubtful and uncertain, though, apparently, without sufficient reason,—see Palmer, *Origines Liturgicæ*, Sect. iii. Vol. i. p. 73. The best edition is that in Goar, *Rituale Græcum*, p. 70—84 (Paris, 1647).

Note E, p. 137.

Echoes of this thought will be found in many of the patristic writers. Evodius, in a letter to Augustine, mentions a story told him by a 'vir quidam sanctus presbyter,' who reported that he had seen 'multitudinem talium de baptisterio exeuntium in corporibus lucidis et postea in medio ipsius ecclesiæ orationes adverterit,' and notices it as a prevailing belief 'in locis in quibus humata corpora sunt, et maxime in basilicis, fieri tumultus et orationes,' *Epist.* clviii. 8, Vol. ii. p. 696. The story of the vision of the ancient man related by Chrysostom in his treatise *de Sacerdot.* (vi. 4) will, I dare say, be remembered by many. To *press* such statements would obviously be the height of folly; but that such sentiments have been privately entertained by many grave thinkers in the early Church, cannot be denied.

Note F, p. 139.

Statements such as that in the text must be accepted only as the expressions of an opinion that seems connected with some of the purest and most indestructible sympathies of our nature. I cannot forbear quoting the following words from Augustine : ' Numquid etiam de his quæ in suis post mortem cujusque contingunt ullus mortuos tangit dolor? Aut hæc saltem scire putandi sunt, quorum sensus alibi est pro meritis seu bene seu male? Cui respondeo magnam quidem esse quæstionem, nec in præsentia disserendum quod sid operis prolixioris, utrum, vel quatenus, vel quomodo ea quæ circa nos aguntur, noverint spiritus mortuorum. Veruntamen, quod breviter dici potest, si nulla illis esset cura de nobis, non diceret Dominus dixisse illum divitem qui tormenta apud inferos patiebatur; *Habeo ibi quinque fratres ne et ipsi veniant in locum hunc tormentorum.'—Enarr.* in *Psalm* cviii. 17, Vol. iv. p. 1437 (ed. Migne). I hope my more sympathizing readers have not forgotten Dr. Johnson's Prayer (*Life*, A.D. 1752) nor the exquisite ballad by Longfellow, entitled, *Footsteps of Angels.*

NOTE G, p. 141.

For a brief consideration of the text here alluded to, see *Commentary in loc.* The majority of modern interpreters seem to incline to the view noticed in the text. To found doctrines, however, on such very doubtful passages, cannot be too emphatically condemned.

NOTE H, p. 142.

For examples of prayers of the unauthorized and perilous kind here alluded to, see Usher, *Answer to a Jesuit*, Vol. iii. p. 215 sq. (ed. Elrington). The general question 'An mortuis prosit oblatio' is discussed by Augustine, and thus decided: 'Non omnibus prosunt, et quare non omnibus prosunt, nisi propter differentiam vitæ quam quisque gessit in corpore?'—*de Dulcit. Quæst.* qu. ii. Vol. vi. p. 157.

NOTE I, p. 142.

The objections of Aerius will be found in Usher, p. 258. Though Aerius was undoubtedly right in many of his views respecting prayers for the dead, he was still a man in favour of whom but little can be said. His behaviour to his friend Eustathius, afterwards Bishop of Sebaste, is apparently indefensible; and it may be, perhaps, not wholly uncharitable to say, that much of the bitterness of his attack on the received ceremonies and discipline of the Church was owing to diappointed ambition; see Epiphanius, *adv. Hær.* lxxv.

Note J, p. 143.

The forms of prayer contained in the first book of Edward VI., both in the Communion and Burial Service, will be found in Keeling, *Liturgies*, p. 210, 335, 341. The year preceding (A.D. 1547), the following was the direction for the bidding-prayer: 'Thirdly, ye shall pray for all them that be departed out of this world in the faith of Christ, that they with us, and we with them, at the day of Judgment, may rest both body and soul with Abraham, Isaac, and Jacob, in the kingdom of heaven,' *Injunctions by Edward VI.*, 1547; see Cardwell's *Documentary Annals*, Vol. i. p. 21 sq. Though these words and the prayers alluded to are couched in language of great sobriety, no reasonable man can doubt, that our Church showed great wisdom in omitting them in the subsequent prayer-books; see Palmer, *Origines Liturgicæ*, Vol. ii. p. 95 sq.

Note K, p. 144.

Prayers of a kind somewhat analogous to the form of the bidding-prayer quoted in the last note, are still used in some of the services at the Commemorations of Benefactors in different Colleges. They are, however, all very cautiously worded, and could not by any distortion be forced into yielding countenance to the doctrine of Purgatory. They are little more than expressions of prayerful hope. It is apparently not to be denied that such expressions have been tolerated long after the Reformation. The reader who has any curiosity about such things, will find them scrupulously enumerated in a work entitled *Hierurgia Anglicana*, p. 320 sq.

With regard to the exercise of this practice *in private*, much may be said on both sides. On the one hand, it is perfectly certain that some of the most loyal members of the Church of England have not scrupled to follow the practice; on the other hand, the weighty remembrance that man is no καρδιογνώστης, and cannot possibly know the exact spiritual state in which those for whom he may desire to pray left this earth, seems to urge on us the most trembling caution, and to bid us to ponder well both the Majesty of God and the true nature of Prayer, before we allow, even in our closets, the perhaps irrepressible uprisings of hope, sympathy, and love, to pass into the definite accents of *prayer*. What we might pray for, in reference to our departed brethren, might conceivably be such as not only could never be granted, but such as might even be in the highest degree unmeet to form the substance of a prayer to an all-merciful, and yet all-just God.

THE END.

BY THE SAME AUTHOR.

HISTORICAL LECTURES ON THE LIFE OF OUR LORD JESUS CHRIST.

BEING THE HULSEAN LECTURES FOR THE YEAR 1859.

Second Edition, 8vo, 10s. 6d.

A CRITICAL AND GRAMMATICAL COMMENTARY ON ST. PAUL'S EPISTLES.

Second Edition, Enlarged.

I. GALATIANS. 8s. 6d.
II. EPHESIANS. 8s. 6d.
III. PASTORAL EPISTLES. 10s. 6d.
IV. PHILIPPIANS, COLOSSIANS, and PHILEMON. 10s. 6d.
V. THESSALONIANS. 7s. 6d.

STANDARD EDITIONS

PRINTED FOR

PARKER, SON, AND BOURN, 445, WEST STRAND,

LONDON.

History of Normandy and of England. By Sir FRANCIS PALGRAVE, Deputy Keeper of the Records. Octavo. Vols. I. and II. 21s. each.

History of England from the Fall of Wolsey to the Death of Elizabeth. By JAMES ANTHONY FROUDE. The Second Edition. Octavo. Volumes I to IV. 54s. These Volumes complete the reign of Henry the Eighth. Vols. V. and VI. containing the Reigns of Edward the Sixth and Mary. 28s.

The Pilgrim: a Dialogue on the Life and Actions of King Henry the Eighth. By WILLIAM THOMAS, Clerk of the Council to Edward VI. Edited, with Notes, from the Archives at Paris and Brussels, by J. A. FROUDE. Octavo. 6s. 6d.

History of England during the Reign of George the Third. By WILLIAM MASSEY, M.P. Octavo. Vols. I., II., and III. 12s. each.

History of Trial by Jury. By WILLIAM FORSYTH, M.A. Octavo. 8s. 6d.

History of the Whig Administration of 1830. By JOHN ARTHUR ROEBUCK, M.P. Octavo. Two Vols. 28s.

The Spanish Conquest in America, and its Relation to the History of Slavery and to the Government of Colonies. By ARTHUR HELPS. Complete in Four Volumes. Octavo. Vols. I., II., 28s.; Vol. III., 16s.; Vol. IV., 16s.

History of Civilization in England. By HENRY THOMAS BUCKLE. The First Volume. Octavo. Third Edition. 21s.

    The Second Volume, containing the History of Civilization in Spain and Scotland. Octavo. 16s.

Revolutions in English History. By ROBERT VAUGHAN, D.D. The First Volume, *Revolutions of Race*. Octavo. 15s.

    The Second Volume, *Revolutions in Religion*. Octavo. 15s.

Studies and Illustrations of the 'Great Rebellion.' By J. LANGTON SANFORD. Octavo. 16s.

The Holy City; Historical, Topographical, and Antiquarian Notices of Jerusalem. By G. WILLIAMS, B.D. Second Edition, with Illustrations and Additions, and a Plan of Jerusalem. Two Vols. £2 5s.

History of the Holy Sepulchre. By PROFESSOR WILLIS. Reprinted from WILLIAM'S *Holy City*. With Illustrations. 9s.

Plan of Jerusalem, from the Ordnance Survey. With a Memoir. 9s.; mounted on rollers, 18s.

The Roman Empire of the West: Four Lectures, by RICHARD CONGREVE, M.A., late Fellow and Tutor of Wadham College, Oxford. Post Octavo. 4s.

The Armenian Origin of the Etruscans. By ROBERT ELLIS, B.D., Fellow of St. John's College, Cambridge; and Author of "A Treatise on Hannibal's Passage of the Alps." Demy Octavo. 7s. 6d.

The Earliest Inhabitants of Italy. From Mommsen's *Roman History*. By G. ROBERTSON. Octavo. 2s.

Claudius Ptolemy and the Nile. By WILLIAM DESBOROUGH COOLEY. Octavo. With a Map. 4s.

The Earth and Man; or, Physical Geography in its Relation to the History of Mankind. From the Work of GUYOT, with Notes and Copious Index. Cheap Edition, 2s.

Hellas: the Home, the History, the Literature, and the Arts of the Ancient Greeks. From the German of JACOBS. Foolscap Octavo. 4s. 6d.

A History of the Literature of Greece. By Professor MÜLLER and Dr. DONALDSON, from the Manuscripts of the late K. O. MÜLLER. The first half of the Translation by the Right Hon. Sir GEORGE CORNEWALL LEWIS, Bart., M.P. The remainder of the Translation, and the completion of the Work according to the Author's plan, by JOHN WILLIAM DONALDSON, D.D. Octavo. Three Vols. 36s. The new portion separately. Two Vols. 20s.

By John William Donaldson, D.D.

Varronianus; a Critical and Historical Introduction to the Ethnography of Ancient Italy, and the Philological Study of the Latin Language. Third Edition. 16s.

The New Cratylus; Contributions towards a more accurate Knowledge of the Greek Language. Third Edition. Revised throughout and considerably enlarged. 20s.

Homeric Ballads: the Greek Text, with an English Translation in Verse, and Introduction and Notes. By Dr. Maginn. Small Octavo. 6s.

Modern Painting at Naples. By Lord Napier. Foolscap Octavo. 4s. 6d.

Principles of Imitative Art. By George Butler, M.A. Post Octavo. 6s.

From the German of Becker.

Charicles: a Tale Illustrative of Private Life among the Ancient Greeks. New Edition, collated and enlarged. 10s. 6d.

Gallus; Roman Scenes of the Time of Augustus. Second Edition, enlarged. With additional Illustrations. 12s.

By William Stirling, M.P.

Cloister Life of the Emperor Charles the Fifth. Third Edition. 8s.

A Long Vacation in Continental Picture Galleries. By T. W. Jex Blake, M.A. Foolscap Octavo. 3s. 6d.

The Young Officer's Companion. By Major-General Lord De Ros. Second Edition. 6s.

Twelve Years of a Soldier's Life in India. Extracts from Letters of Major Hodson, Commandant of Hodson's Horse; Edited by his Brother, the Rev. George H. Hodson, M.A. Third Edition, with Additions. 10s. 6d.

By Harris Prendergast, Barrister-at-Law.

The Law relating to Officers in the Army. Revised Edition. 6s. 6d.

The Law relating to Officers of the Navy. In Two Parts. 10s. 6d.

By the Right Hon. Sir G. Cornewall Lewis, Bart., M.P.

A Historical Survey of the Astronomy of the Ancients.

An Enquiry into the Credibility of the Early Roman History. Octavo. Two Vols. 30s.

On the Use and Abuse of Certain Political Terms. Octavo. 9s. 6d.

On the Methods of Observation and Reasoning in Politics. Octavo. Two Vols. 28s.

On the Influence of Authority in Matters of Opinion. Octavo. 10s. 6d.

On Foreign Jurisdiction and the Extradition of Criminals. Octavo. 2s. 6d.

George Canning and his Times. By Augustus Granville Stapleton. Octavo. 16s.

Oxford Essays. By Members of the University. Four Volumes, 7s. 6d. each.

Cambridge Essays. By Members of the University. Four Volumes, 7s. 6d. each.

By the Author of 'Friends in Council.'

Friends in Council. A New Series. Two Volumes. Post Octavo. 14s.

Friends in Council. First Series. New Edition. Two Volumes. 9s.

Companions of my Solitude. Fifth Edition. 3s. 6d.

Essays written in the Intervals of Business. Seventh Edition. 2s. 6d.

On Taxation: how it is raised and how it is expended. By Leone Levi, Professor of Commercial Law in King's College, London. Post Octavo. 7s. 6d.

The Recreations of a Country Parson. Being a Selection from the Contributions of A. K. H. B. to *Fraser's Magazine*. First Series. Third Edition. Crown Octavo. 9s. Second Series. Crown Octavo, 9s.

By John Stuart Mill.

Considerations on Representative Government. Second Edition. Octavo. 9s.

Dissertations and Discussions, Political, Philosophical, and Historical. 24s.

Thoughts on Parliamentary Reform. Second Edition, with Supplement. 1s. 6d.

On Liberty. Second Edition. 7s. 6d.

Principles of Political Economy. Fourth Edition. Two Volumes. 30s.

A System of Logic, Ratiocinative and Inductive. Fourth Edition. Two Volumes. 25s.

By Alex. Bain, M.A., Professor of Logic in the University of Aberdeen, and Examiner in Logic and Moral Philosophy in the University of London.

On the Study of Character, including an Estimate of Phrenology. Octavo. 9s.

The Senses and the Intellect. Octavo. 15s.

The Emotions and the Will: completing a Systematic Exposition of the Human Mind. Octavo. 15s.

Dialogues on Divine Providence. By a Fellow of a College. Foolscap Octavo. 3s. 6d.

God's Acre; or, Historical Notices relating to Churchyards. By Mrs. Stone. Post Octavo. 10s. 6d.

Transactions of the National Association for the Promotion of Social Science. 1859, 16s. 1860, 12s.

The Institutes of Justinian; with English Introduction, Translation, and Notes. By Thomas C. Sandars, M.A., Late Fellow of Oriel College, Oxford. Octavo. 15s.

Principles and Maxims of Jurisprudence. By J. G. Phillimore, Q.C., Reader to the Four Inns of Court. Octavo. 12s.

De Lolme's Rise and Progress of the English Constitution. With Historical and Legal Introduction and Notes by A. J. Stephens, LL.D., F.R.S. Two Volumes. Octavo. £1 10s.

Statutes relating to the Ecclesiastical Institutions of England, India, and the Colonies; with the Decisions thereon. By Archibald J. Stephens, LL.D., F.R.S. Two Volumes, Royal Octavo. £3 3s.

Charges on the Administration of the Criminal Law, the Repression of Crime, and the Reformation of Offenders. By Matthew Davenport Hill, Q.C., Recorder of Birmingham. Octavo. 16s.

Remains of Bishop Copleston. With Reminiscences of his Life. By the Archbishop of Dublin. With Portrait. 10s. 6d.

Memoir of Bishop Copleston. By W. J. Copleston, M.A. Octavo. 10s. 6d.

Essays and Remains of the Rev. Robert Alfred Vaughan. With a Memoir by R. Vaughan, D.D. Two Vols., with Portrait. 14s.

English Life, Social and Domestic, in the Nineteenth Century. Third Edition, Revised. 4s. 6d.

Evelyn's Life of Mrs. Godolphin; Edited by the Bishop of Oxford. Third Edition, with Portrait. 6s.

The Merchant and the Friar; Truths and Fictions of the Middle Ages. An Historical Tale. By Sir Francis Palgrave. Second Edition. 3s.

By William George Clark, M.A., Public Orator, Cambridge.

Peloponnesus: Notes of Study and Travel. Octavo. With Maps. 10s. 6d.

Gazpacho; or, Summer Months in Spain. New and Cheaper Edition. 5s.

The Mediterranean: a Memoir, Physical, Historical, and Nautical. By Admiral W. H. Smyth, F.R.S., &c. Octavo. 15s.

Tour in the Crimea, and other Countries adjacent to the Black Sea. By Lord De Ros. Crown Octavo. 4s. 6d.

A Manual of Geographical Science, Mathematical, Physical, Historical, and Descriptive. In Two Parts.

PART I. comprises
MATHEMATICAL GEOGRAPHY. By the late Professor M. O'BRIEN.
PHYSICAL GEOGRAPHY. By D. T. ANSTED, M.A., F.R.S.
CHARTOGRAPHY. By J. R. JACKSON, F.R.S.
THEORY OF DESCRIPTION AND GEOGRAPHICAL TERMINOLOGY. By the Rev. C. G. NICOLAY.

PART II. contains
ANCIENT GEOGRAPHY. By the Rev. W. L. BEVAN.
MARITIME DISCOVERY AND MODERN GEOGRAPHY. By the Rev. C. G. NICOLAY.

And a copious Index to the whole Work. Two closely-printed Volumes, Octavo, with many Woodcuts, 25s. 6d. The Parts separately. Part I., 10s. 6d.; Part II., 15s.

An Atlas of Physical and Historical Geography. Engraved by J. W. LOWRY, under the direction of Professor ANSTED and the Rev. C. G. NICOLAY.

CONTENTS:—
1. Reference Map.—The World on Mercator's Projection.
2. Meteorological Map of the World.
3. Relief Map of the World, showing the Elevations of the Earth's Surface.
4. Phytographical Map, showing the Distribution of Plants in the World.
   Vertical Distribution of Plants and Animals.
5. Zoological Map, showing the Distribution of Animals in the World.
   Ethnographical Map, showing the Distribution of the Races of Men.
6. Chart of Ancient and Modern Geography and Geographical Discoveries.

Imperial Folio, in a Wrapper, 5s.

This Atlas was constructed with an especial view to the above Manual, but will be found a valuable companion to Works on Geography in General.

The Military Topography of Continental Europe. From the French of M. Th. Lavallée. By Col. J. R. JACKSON, F.R.S., &c. 8s.

The Kingdom and People of Siam; With a Narrative of the Mission to that Country in 1855. By Sir JOHN BOWRING, F.R.S., her Majesty's Plenipotentiary in China. Two Vols., with Illustrations and Map. 32s.

A Year with the Turks. By WARINGTON W. SMYTH, M.A. With a Coloured Ethnographical Map by LOWRY. Crown Octavo. 8s.

The Biographical History of Philosophy, from its origin in Greece down to the present day. By GEORGE HENRY LEWES. Library Edition. Octavo. 16s.

Paley's Evidences of Christianity. With Annotations by the ARCHBISHOP OF DUBLIN. Octavo, 9s.

Paley's Moral Philosophy, with Annotations by RICHARD WHATELY, D.D., Archbishop of Dublin. Octavo. 7s.

Bacon's Essays, with Annotations by Archbishop WHATELY. Fifth Edition. Octavo. 10s. 6d.

By RICHARD CHENEVIX TRENCH, D.D., Dean of Westminster.

A Select Glossary of English Words used formerly in Senses different from their present. Second Edition. 4s.

English, Past and Present. Fourth Edition. 4s.

Proverbs and their Lessons. Fifth Edition. 3s.

On the Study of Words. Tenth Edition. 3s. 6d.

On Deficiencies in our English Dictionaries. Second Edition. Octavo. 3s.

State Papers and Correspondence, illustrative of the State of Europe, from the Revolution to the Accession of the House of Hanover; with Introduction, Notes, and Sketches. By JOHN M. KEMBLE, M.A. Octavo. 16s.

On the Classification and Geographical Distribution of the Mammalia: being the Lecture on Sir Robert Reade's Foundation, delivered before the University of Cambridge, 1859; with an Appendix on the Gorilla, and on the Extinction and Transmutation of Species. By RICHARD OWEN, F.R.S., Superintendent of the Natural History Department in the British Museum. Octavo. 5s.

Leaves from the Note-Book of a Naturalist. By W. J. BRODERIP, F.R.S. Post Octavo. 10s. 6d.

Familiar History of Birds. By Bishop STANLEY. Cheaper Edition. 3s. 6d.

By **William Whewell, D.D., F.R.S.,** Master of Trinity Coll., Camb.

History of the Inductive Sciences. Third Edition. Three Vols. 24s.

History of Scientific Ideas: being the First Part of a Newly Revised Edition of the *Philosophy of the Inductive Sciences.* Small Octavo. Two Vols. 14s.

Novum Organon Renovatum: being the Second Part of a Newly Revised Edition of the *Philosophy of the Inductive Sciences.* Small Octavo. 7s.

On the Philosophy of Discovery, Chapters Historical and Critical, being the third and concluding Part of the Revised Edition of the *Philosophy of the Inductive Sciences.* 9s.

Indications of the Creator. Second Edition. 5s. 6d.

Elements of Morality; including Polity. Two Vols. Third Edition. 15s.

Lectures on Systematic Morality. Octavo. 7s. 6d.

Of a Liberal Education in General. Part I., 4s. 6d.; Part II., 3s. 6d.; Part III., 2s.

On the Principles of English University Education. Octavo. 5s.

Architectural Notes on German Churches. Third Edition. Octavo. 12s.

By **Mary Roberts.**

Wild Animals; and the Regions they Inhabit. Cheaper Edition. 2s. 6d.

Domesticated Animals; with reference to Civilization. Cheaper Edition. 2s. 6d.

By **Emily Shirreff.**

Why should we Learn? Short Lectures addressed to Schools. Foolscap Octavo. 2s.

A System of Surgery, Theoretical and Practical, in Treatises by various Authors, arranged and edited by T. Holmes, M.A. Cantab, Surgeon to the Hospital for Sick Children, and Assistant-Surgeon to St. George's Hospital. Volume I. General Pathology. Demy 8vo, £1 1s. Volume II. Local Injuries: Diseases of the Eye. Demy Octavo. £1 1s.

Lectures on the Principles and Practice of Physic. By Thomas Watson, M.D., Physician Extraordinary to the Queen. Fourth Edition, revised. Two Volumes. Octavo. 34s.

By **Henry Gray, F.R.S.,** Lecturer on Anatomy at St. George's Hospital.

Anatomy, Descriptive and Surgical. With nearly 400 large Woodcuts, from original Drawings, from Dissections made by the Author and Dr. Carter. Royal Octavo, Second Edition. 28s.

The Structure and Use of the Spleen. With 64 Illustrations. 15s.

Physiological Anatomy and Physiology of Man. By Robert Bentley Todd, M.D., F.R.S., and William Bowman, F.R.S., of King's College. With numerous Original Illustrations. Two Volumes. £2.

Manual of Human Microscopic Anatomy. By Albert Kolliker. With numerous Illustrations. Octavo. 24s.

On Spasm, Languor, and Palsy. By J. A. Wilson, M.D. Post Octavo. 7s.

By **George Johnson, M.D.,** Physician to King's College Hospital.

On the Diseases of the Kidney; their Pathology, Diagnosis, and Treatment. Octavo. With Illustrations. 14s.

On Epidemic Diarrhœa and Cholera; their Pathology and Treatment. With a Record of Cases. Crown Octavo. 7s. 6d.

Lunacy and Lunatic Life: with Hints on Management. Small Octavo. 3s. 6d.

On Medical Testimony and Evidence in Cases of Lunacy; with an Essay on the Conditions of Mental Soundness. By Thomas Mayo, M.D., F.R.S., President of the Royal College of Physicians. Foolscap Octavo. 3s. 6d.

Diphtheria: its History and Treatment. By E. Headlam Greenhow, M.D., Fellow of the Royal College of Physicians. Octavo. 7s. 6d.

A Dictionary of Materia Medica and Pharmacy. By William Thomas Brande, F.R.S. Octavo. 15s.

Popular Physiology. By Dr. Lord. Third Edition. 5s.

By **John Tomes, F.R.S.**

On the Use and Management of Artificial Teeth. With Illustrations. 3s. 6d.

German Mineral Waters; and their employment in certain Chronic Diseases. By Sigismund Sutro, M.D., Senior Physician of the German Hospital. Foolscap Octavo. 7s. 6d.

By William Allen Miller, M.D., F.R.S., Professor of Chemistry, King's College, London.

Elements of Chemistry, Theoretical and Practical. With numerous Illustrations. Part I. Chemical Physics. Second Edition. 10s. 6d. Part II. Inorganic Chemistry. Second Edition. 20s. Part III. Organic Chemistry. Second Edition. 20s.

First Lines in Chemistry for Beginners. By Dr. Albert J. Bernays, F.C.S., Lecturer on Chemistry at St. Mary's Hospital. With Illustrations. 7s.

The Chemistry of the Four Ancient Elements—Fire, Air, Earth, and Water: an Essay founded upon Lectures delivered before her Majesty the Queen. By Thomas Griffiths. Second Edition. 4s. 6d.

Of the Plurality of Worlds. An Essay. Fifth Edition. 6s.

Lectures on Astronomy, delivered at King's College, London. By Henry Moseley, M.A., F.R.S., one of her Majesty's Inspectors of Schools. Cheaper Edition. 3s. 6d.

Recreations in Astronomy. By the Rev. Lewis Tomlinson. Fourth Edition. 4s. 6d.

By J. Russell Hind, Foreign Secretary of the Royal Astronomical Society of London.

The Comets: with an Account of Modern Discoveries, and a Table of all the Calculated Comets, from the Earliest Ages. Post Octavo. 5s. 6d.

The Comet of 1556: on its anticipated Re-appearance, and on the Apprehension of Danger from Comets. Post Octavo. 2s. 6d.

An Astronomical Vocabulary; an Explanation of all Terms in Use amongst Astronomers. Small Octavo. 1s. 6d.

Elements of Meteorology. By John Frederick Daniell, F.R.S., &c. Two Volumes. With Charts and Plates. 32s.

On the Nature of Thunder-storms; and on the Means of Protecting Buildings and Shipping against the Effects of Lightning. By Sir W. Snow Harris, F.R.S. Octavo. 10s. 6d.

The British Palæozoic Rocks and Fossils. By Professor Sedgwick and Professor M'Coy. Royal Quarto, with numerous Plates. Two Vols. 42s.

By Captain Lendy, Director of the Practical Military College at Sunbury, late of the French Staff.

Elements of Fortification, Field and Permanent. With 236 Woodcuts. 7s. 6d.

The Principles of War; or, Elementary Treatise on the Higher Tactics and Strategy, intended for the use of young Military Students. 5s.

By Butler Williams, C.E.

Practical Geodesy; Chain Surveying, Surveying Instruments, Levelling, Trigonometry, and Mining; Maritime, Estate, Parochial, and Railroad Surveying. Third Edition revised. Octavo. 8s. 6d.

A Manual of Model-Drawing from Solid Forms; with a Popular View of Perspective; Shaded Engravings of the Models, and numerous Woodcuts. Octavo. 15s. This Manual is published under the Sanction of the Committee of Council on Education.

Readings in English Prose Literature; from the Works of the best English Writers; with Essays on English Literature. Fifth Edition. 3s. 6d.

Readings in Poetry; from the Works of the best English Poets, with Specimens of the American Poets. Thirteenth Edition. 3s. 6d.

Readings in Biography; a Selection of the Lives of Eminent Men of all Nations. Fifth Edition. 3s. 6d.

Readings in Science; Familiar Explanations of Appearances and Principles in Natural Philosophy. Fourth Edition. 3s. 6d.

Woman's Rights and Duties, considered with reference to their Effects on Society and on her own Condition. By a Woman.
Two Volumes, Post Octavo. 14s.

Woman's Mission.
The Fourteenth Edition. 2s. 6d.

By John S. B. Monsell, LL.D.

Spiritual Songs for the Sundays and Holydays throughout the Year. Third Edition, revised. 4s. 6d.

His Presence not His Memory. 1s.

The Beatitudes. Abasement before God—Sorrow for Sin—Meekness of Spirit Desire for Holiness—Gentleness—Purity of Heart—The Peacemakers—Sufferings for Christ. By the same Author. Fcap. Octavo. 3s. 6d.

By Coventry Patmore.

Faithful for Ever. Foolscap Octavo. 6s.

The Angel in the House. Part I. The Betrothal. Part II. The Espousals. Cheap Edition, in One Volume. 7s. 6d.

Songs for the Suffering. By Rev. Thomas Davis, M.A. Foolscap Octavo. 4s. 6d.

Cecil and Mary; or, Phases of Life and Love. A Missionary Poem. By Joseph Edward Jackson. Foolscap Octavo. 4s.

Pinocchi, and other Poems. Crown Octavo. 5s.

Days and Hours, and other Poems. By Frederick Tennyson. Foolscap Octavo. 5s.

By the Rev. Charles Kingsley.

Andromeda, and other Poems. Second Edition. 5s.

The Saint's Tragedy: the True Story of Elizabeth of Hungary. Third Edition. 5s.

Oulita, the Serf; a Tragedy. By the Author of *Friends in Council*. 6s.

King Henry the Second. An Historical Drama. 6s.

Nina Sforza. A Tragedy. By R Zouch S. Troughton. Third Edition. 2s.

The Sea Spirit, and other Poems. By Lady Lushington. 4s. 6d.

Arundines Cami, sive Musarum Cantabrigiensium Lusus Canori. Collegit atque edidit Henricus Drury, M.A. Fifth and cheaper Edition. 7s. 6d.

By Richard Chenevix Trench.

Calderon's Life's a Dream: with an Essay on his Life and Genius. 4s. 6d.

Justin Martyr, and other Poems. Fourth Edition. 6s.

Poems from Eastern Sources: Genoveva and other Poems. Second Edition. 5s. 6d.

Elegiac Poems. Third Edition. 2s. 6d.

By Edgar Alfred Bowring.

The Book of Psalms literally rendered into English Verse. Small Octavo. 5s.

The Complete Poems of Schiller, Attempted in English Verse. Foolscap Octavo. 6s.

The Poems of Goethe. Translated in the original Metres. 7s. 6d.

Translated by Theodore Martin.

The Odes of Horace, with a Life and Notes. Second Edition. 9s.

Catullus. Translated into English Verse, with Life and Notes. 6s. 6d.

Aladdin. A Dramatic Poem. By Adam Oehlenschlaeger. 5s.

Correggio. A Tragedy. By Oehlenschlaeger. 3s.

King Rene's Daughter: a Danish Lyrical Drama. By Hinrich Hertz. 2s. 6d.

By the Author of *The Heir of Redclyffe*.

The Young Stepmother; or, a Chronicle of Mistakes. 10s. 6d.

Hopes and Fears; or, Scenes from the Life of a Spinster. Cheap Edition. One Volume. 6s.
Two Vols., Foolscap 8vo, 12s.

The Heir of Redclyffe. Thirteenth Edition. 6s.

Heartsease, or the Brother's Wife. Seventh Edition. 6s.

The Lances of Lynwood. Fourth Edition. 3s.

The Little Duke. Cheap Edition. 1s. 6d.

The Daisy Chain. Cheap Edition. One Volume. 6s.

Dynevor Terrace. Third Edition. 6s.

By G. J. WHYTE MELVILLE.

Good for Nothing; or, All Down Hill. Two Vols. Post 8vo. 16s.

Holmby House: a Tale of Old Northamptonshire. Second Edition. Two Vols. Post 8vo. 16s.

Digby Grand. Third Edition. 5s.

General Bounce. Second and cheaper Edition. 5s.

Kate Coventry, an Autobiography. Third Edition. 5s.

The Interpreter: a Tale of the War. Second Edition. 10s. 6d.

By ANNA HARRIETT DRURY.

Friends and Fortune. Second Edition. 6s.

The Inn by the Sea-Side. An Allegory. Small Octavo. 2s.

The Nut-Brown Maids: a Family Chronicle of the Days of Queen Elizabeth. Post Octavo. 10s. 6d.

My Heart's in the Highlands. By the same. Post Octavo. 10s. 6d.

Meg of Elibank and other Tales. By the same. Post Octavo. 9s.

Wearing the Willow; or, Bride Fielding: a Tale of Ireland and Scotland Sixty Years ago. By the same. Post Octavo. 9s.

Mademoiselle Mori: a Tale of Modern Rome. 6s.

Ballyblunder: an Irish Story. Post 8vo. 6s.

By the Author of *Dorothy*.

Martha Brown, the Heiress. 5s.

Dorothy. A Tale. 4s. 6d.

The Maiden Sisters. 5s.

Still Waters. Two Volumes. 9s.

De Cressy. A Tale. 4s. 6d.

Uncle Ralph. A Tale. 4s. 6d.

Gryll Grange. By the Author of *Headlong Hall*. Small Octavo. 7s. 6d.

Hanworth. A Tale. Small Octavo. 7s. 6d.

The Two Mottoes. A Tale. By the Author of *Summerleigh Manor*. Small Octavo. 5s.

For and Against; or, Queen Margaret's Badge. By FRANCES M. WILBRAHAM. Two Volumes. 10s. 6d.

Likes and Dislikes; or, Passages in the Life of Emily Marsden. Small 8vo. 6s.

Chilcote Park; or, the Sisters. By the same. Foolscap Octavo. 5s.

New Friends: a Tale for Children. By the Author of *Julian and his Playfellows*. Small Octavo. 2s. 6d.

Baby Bianca. A Venetian Story. By Mrs. VALENTINE. Fcap. 8vo. 4s. 6d.

Compensation. A Story of Real Life Thirty Years Ago. Two Volumes. 9s.

By CHARLES KINGSLEY, Rector of Eversley.

Yeast: a Problem. Fourth Edition, with New Preface. 5s.

Hypatia; or, New Foes with an Old Face. Third Edition. 6s.

The Upper Ten Thousand: Sketches of American Society. By A NEW YORKER. Foolscap Octavo. 5s.

Hassan, the Child of the Pyramid; an Egyptian Tale. By the Hon. C. A. MURRAY, C.B. Two Volumes. 21s.

Dauntless. Two Volumes. 8s.

Sword and Gown. By the Author of *Guy Livingstone*. Second and Cheaper Edition. 4s. 6d.

Aggesden Vicarage: a Tale for the Young. Two Volumes, Fap. 8vo. 9s.

Chance and Choice; or, the Education of Circumstances. Post Octavo. 7s. 6d.

Brampton Rectory. Second Edition. 8s. 6d.

Youth and Womanhood of Helen Tyrrel. Post Octavo. 6s.

Compton Merivale. Post Octavo. 8s. 6d.

Opinions on the World, Mankind, Literature, Science, and Art. From the German of Goethe. Foolscap Octavo. 3s. 6d.

Tales from the German of Tieck, containing the 'Old Man of the Mountain,' the 'Love Charm,' and 'Pietro of Abano.' 2s. 6d.

Extracts from the Works of Jean Paul Richter. Translated by LADY CHATTERTON. Foolscap Octavo. 3s. 6d.

www.ingramcontent.com/pod-product-compliance
Lightning Source LLC
Chambersburg PA
CBHW020915230426
43666CB00008B/1461